A JOURNEY THROUGH THE MICHIGAN UNDERWORLD

THE STOOGES

Published in 2008 by
INDEPENDENT MUSIC PRESS
Independent Music Press is an imprint of I.M. P. Publishing Limited
This Work is Copyright © I. M. P. Publishing Ltd 2008

The Stooges – A Journey Through The Michigan Underworld
by Brett Callwood

British Library Cataloguing-in-Publication Data.
A catalogue for this book is available from The British Library.
ISBN: 978-1-906191-01-6 & 1-906191-01-8

Cover Design by Fresh Lemon.
Cover photograph by FotoFest/Retna

Printed in the UK.

Independent Music Press
P.O. Box 69,
Church Stretton, Shropshire
SY6 6WZ
Visit us on the web at: www.impbooks.com
and www.myspace.com/independentmusicpress
For a free catalogue, e-mail us at: info@impbooks.com
Fax: 01694 720049

A JOURNEY THROUGH THE MICHIGAN UNDERWORLD

THE STOOGES

BRETT CALLWOOD

Independent Music Press

ACKNOWLEDGEMENTS

It may be my name on the cover, but the following people made this book possible. Obviously, there'd be no Stooges book without The Stooges, so a big thank you to Ron Asheton, Steve Mackay, Mike Watt, James Williamson and Iggy Pop for speaking with me. Thanks also to Scott Asheton and Dave Alexander (RIP) for living such interesting lives.

To Niagara and Colonel Galaxy, Ron Cooke, Johnny Bee, Jerry Vile, Russ Gibb, Michael Davis, Dennis Thompson, John Sinclair, J Mascis, Hiawatha Bailey, Gary Rasmussen, Scott Morgan, The Farleys, Jimmy Doom, Mique Craig, Chris Marlow, Pete Bankert, Shaun Claydon Carroll and Tom Gardener – thanks for the interviews in Detroit and on the phone.

Paul Trynka – thanks for the Cheatham interview; Steve Zuccaro and Ashley Petz – thanks for lending me your spare room for two weeks; Scotty Ross, Anthony Brancaleone (A Detroit Thing), Paul Lamb, Paul Randolph, Professor Chuck, Richard Peardon, the Lions and the Tigers (both of whom gave me a live win), Gusoline Alley (my new favourite bar), Karen Neal, Kimmy Anne Leitz-McCauley and everyone at the Detroit Erotica Ball (strange night); Dino Zoyes, Dave Allison, Kathy Vargo and Blender Detroit, Becca and Stephanie Tyler, Hedda Hart, Melissa Miller, Marvin's Mechanical Museum, everyone at the Whitby Gothic Weekend and Dingo; Mike Fury and everyone at the Rock Action Fest.

Carla Eden for the Myspace support and everyone else that reads the nonsense that I post on there. (Tempted? Find me at *www.myspace.com/brettcallwood*); John Holmstrom, Spencer Weisberg, Scott Nydegger, Howard Wuelfing and Philippe Mogane; The People's Art's Festival, George Clinton, Rilo Kiley, Bulldog, The Black Lips, Ani DiFranco, The Heart Attacks and the

Subhumans for keeping me entertained in Michigan; my friends in Crud: David Black, Vinnie Dombroski, Dana Forrester, my brother Eric Hoegemeyer and Danielle Arsenault; Mum, Dad, Scott, Corinne Quail, Chris Mann and Toni Deville – thanks for all of the support.

Thanks to Martin and Dave at Independent Music Press.

And to anyone I may have forgotten ... I apologise because, to quote Iggy, my mind's Swiss cheese.

CONTENTS

INTRODUCTION

The title of this book is *The Stooges: A Journey Through The Michigan Underworld*, but it could just as easily be called *The Detroit Chronicles, Part II*. During 2006, I wrote my first book, *Sonically Speaking*, a biography of the MC5. While often gruelling and always incredibly hard work, the experience was ultimately an uplifting and inspiring one. When the reviews that followed were almost all glowing (with a couple of obligatory exceptions), I found that I had developed confidence as a writer that my journalistic commitments could never give me. With a book on the shelves, even my mum was proud.

And so, with the MC5 saga put to bed, at least in literary terms, it was time to think about book number two, but really there was little to think about. I believe The Stooges' story is one that needs to be told. Or at least, it needs to be told in the way that I would want to read it.

Around the same time that Independent Music Press put out my MC5 biography, former *Mojo* editor Paul Trynka released a biography of Iggy Pop, called *Open Up And Bleed*. It's a fantastic book, totally deserving of the praise that it received from all sides. It covers Iggy's short time with The Stooges in great detail, and all fans of both Iggy and The Stooges should certainly own a copy. But I wanted to do something different. My approach, put simply, was to treat the Asheton brothers, Ron and Scott, with the same amount of respect as their singer. I wanted to know all about former members Dave Alexander and James Williamson, as well as new boy Mike Watt and perennial sax man Steve Mackay. I wanted to know what these guys had done pre-and-post-Stooges, and I wanted to give those stories more coverage than another anecdote about what Iggy did with Bowie in Berlin. I wanted to treat The Stooges as a band, rather than as something that Iggy Pop once did. What started as a germ of an idea in the back of my mind started to grow and spread while interviewing Mudhoney man Mark Arm for my MC5 book. Mentioning my plans for a Stooges book that focussed on the Ashetons, Arm said to me that, "it's a forgotten story."

Of course, there was always going to be some crossover, both with my own MC5 book, and with Trynka's excellent Iggy biography, not to mention the countless other Iggy books that are on the shelves. When guitarist Fred Smith came out of the Motor City 5, he formed the Sonic's Rendezvous Band, featuring Scott Asheton on drums. Similarly, both Dennis Thompson and Mike Davis of the MC5 played in bands with Ron Asheton (the former in The New Order and the latter in Destroy All Monsters). The trick, however, would be to tell these stories from the perspective of the Stooges' men. This book has been designed to sit comfortably alongside the aforementioned chronicles, by simply but quite deliberately shifting the focus.

As I was coming to the end of *Sonically Speaking*, I wrote, "After speaking to Dennis Thompson, Michael Davis and Wayne Kramer, I realised that I had been spoiled. When I come to write my second book, whomever it shall be about, surely I'll never be treated so well and openly again." As prophecies go, this one was a bit of a corker. While the MC5 pretty much made themselves available on tap to me for interviews, the Asheton brothers were more difficult to get hold of, verging on being reclusive, or at least elusive. Add this to the fact that while I had written the first proper MC5 biography, The Stooges had had many pages already written about them, and it was obvious from the start that this was going to be a different beast entirely. The upside was that, because of the countless existing Iggy Pop biographies, I was free to put whatever slant I wanted on to my book, and not be accused of missing out major parts of the story.

I visited Detroit for two weeks on a research mission during September 2007. Very quickly it became obvious that, if I was going to be able to talk with the Asheton brothers, it was going to take some time and a lot of persuading. Therefore, while in Detroit, I spoke with a lot of people that had played a part in The Stooges' history, people that impacted on the lives of these men, or had been impacted upon by them. The adventures that I had along the way began to form a story of their own, and so the focus of my book began to shift once more. Detroit, and more accurately, Ann Arbor, is rightfully proud of The Stooges and the coverage that the band has given to their city, and it was the people that I spoke to along my drunken two-week journey that I began to find interesting. This band had changed the city; there is an underground music scene still blossoming that The Stooges have had a profound effect upon. So that's where the title of the book comes from. I thought I'd seen everything until I ventured to Detroit for this trip. I don't know whether it was the length of my stay this time around or the band that I was researching, but the mere mention of The Stooges seemed to inspire chaos in Detroit, much of which has been documented in these pages. You're about to meet Ron Cooke and Johnny Bee, former members of both The Detroit Wheels and The Detroit band and two extremely funny gentlemen. Then there's Jerry Vile, former member of The Boners and one-time editor of the infamous *Orbit* magazine. Jerry gave me an afternoon I'll never forget. My evening at the Detroit Erotica Ball is chronicled, a night of utter debauchery that even Iggy would surely have winced at. I had two meetings with the fabulous Niagara, former front-woman with Destroy All Monsters, and her husband Colonel Galaxy, and both were of huge importance to my understanding of what makes Ron Asheton tick. And then there was the premiere of the *A Detroit Thing* movie, a film that documents the Detroit music scene over the last 15 years. Watching the many bands that appear on screen during the course of the film, it's impossible to ignore the impact that The Stooges had on just about every one of them.

These experiences became vital to my journey of discovery, trying to find the real Stooges, and so they each get a short chapter in between the main chapters that document the history of the band. There are other events that occurred while there that didn't warrant a section of their own, but are possibly worth mentioning so I have included the diary of my trip, updated daily during my time there, at the back of the book. It may turn out to be of interest to no-one but me, but it's an honest account of what got me to the stage where I was able to write the very book you are now holding.

Niagara also gave me the phone number of a guy called Hiawatha Bailey, singer in The Cult Heroes and an old friend of The Stooges. As well as granting me an interview himself, Hiawatha proved to be invaluable in helping me get in contact with all manner of people who had, in some small part, come into contact with The Stooges over the years. Thanks to him, I spoke to a lady named Mique Craig, an Ann Arbor party girl in the 70s. Hiawatha also put me in touch with Pete Bankert, who had played in Dark Carnival with Ron, and Shaun Carroll, who himself had hung around with the Ashetons at The Second Chance club in Ann Arbor during the Destroy All Monsters/Sonic's Rendezvous Band days.

After months of chasing, I finally spoke to Ron Asheton for the first time a mere four weeks before deadline. After obtaining his home phone number, I had been leaving messages on his answering machine for about a week before he picked up. At the time, he was slogging through his tax return but we arranged an interview for the following week (three weeks before deadline, for those keeping count). Ron told me that he thought I'd done a great job with the MC5 book, and that he would be glad to give me some of his time. I was already most of the way into writing what I considered to be a strong book, but Ron's additions would surely prove integral.

The day after I spoke with Ron, I received an email from Iggy saying that he too would be happy to speak with me, though he stated certain conditions. The email read: "Dear Brett, I have been planning for some time to give you a call off the cuff during the last week in November. My schedule has been unexpectedly busy … I have some questions about what you're doing. I read quite a bit of your MC5 work on an airplane with Ron. I found it sincere and straightforward. There may be things I don't want to talk to you about and I may want to ask you for some questions or subjects in advance of an actual interview. I am very glad that someone is writing a book about Ron and Scott. They are truly amazing people, and fine musicians. Best, Iggy Pop"

Just like the buses, I was waiting for months for Iggy and Ronnie to get back to me, and then they both did so within a day of each other. Still, I was thrilled at the idea of Iggy and Ron sat on an airplane looking through my MC5 book, and thrilled further that they both liked it. My desire to do them justice in print was only furthered.

On the 26th November 2007, I was on my way into London on the train, when my phone buzzed to tell me that I had a voicemail. It was from Iggy Pop. This is what he said:

"Hey Brett, it's Iggy. It's 11.36am Eastern Standard Time, and I'm calling you to get in touch. I'll be with Spencer, my assistant, until about 1pm or shortly thereafter. I'll be back here later, and I'll try to call you again or you can try to call me back on this number. I'm gonna get beat up at the dentist (laughs), in the midst of the afternoon so, ahh, don't expect, ahh, to, umm, well, (laughs hard), oh, you know. Bye bye."

Obviously, I called him back immediately and was delighted to finally speak to him. Iggy told me once again that he had liked my MC5 book, and that he was keen to be involved in my project. I had already sent him some questions in advance, but he also asked me to email him a sentence or two about where I was coming from with this project – why I wanted to write about The Stooges, and The Ashetons in particular. This I did, and then I found out that The Stooges were on tour in the States for a week, so I had to wait it out once again.

On the 18th November, 2007, I attended the first annual Rock Action Festival at Bar Monsta in Camden, London. Celebrating all things punk and garage rock, local bands like The Vermin and The Moon appeared and the low-key event was a success. A minor success, but a success all the same. I was there to give away three signed copies of my MC5 biography *Sonically Speaking* in a raffle. The whole thing became much more important, however, when talking with Mike Fury, one of the organisers and drummer with the band Bubblegum Screw. Mike told me that he was friends with someone who worked closely with former Stooges James Williamson. At that point, my efforts to get in contact with Williamson had proved fruitless and I had all but given up, but Fury had opened the door a crack and I suddenly had a way in.

I emailed Mike's contact, a French guy by the name of Philippe Mogane, at the next available opportunity, and Mogane soon got back to me with the following reply:

"Hi Brett,
Thanks for your exciting message.
Did you read the latest book: *Open Up And Bleed*? I helped Paul with his book.
I will be more than happy to help you out.
James and I started Siamese Records (which begins anew, for the Millennium, under the name of Siamese Dogs Records) in April 1977 and released a monster hit, 'I Got A Right'.
Then, James went on to a Sound Engineer school and left me with the label to run … in fact, it was a blessing as I discovered that I could be a Producer.

And in parallel to Photography (I was representing European magazines and a Japanese agency), I signed acts who became real famous, like The Controllers and The Weasels, and I still do.

Lately, I have signed new acts: Mickey Finn & Chris Lynn (typical English Blues rock), In Vitro (French rock band) and a new power trio from NYC, P.L.M.B., with who we are presently touring and who's getting a lot of attention in France.

I am sorry to have kept you reading all those lines but I needed to let you know my connections and the work we did with James.

I am very much in touch with him and I insisted to have him appear in a documentary about *The Stooges: Once A Stooge, Always A Stooge.*

I couldn't stand having a documentary on The Stooges, which didn't include James Williamson.

I am the first guardian of his rights and fame. Let me know what you have in mind and I will pass it on to him. He lives around the San Francisco area. But he does come to the south of France once in a while.

Anyway, I leave you to your chores.

Keep in touch and thank you again for your interest.

Rockably Yours,

Philippe Mogane

Producer/Publisher."

Philippe introduced my project to Williamson, and before long James had given Philippe permission to give me his email. Detroit is very much Ron's town and understandably so. But when speaking with James, even after a slightly difficult start, I found him to be charming and immediately likable. James turned out to be warm and sharp, and very witty. The anecdotes that he provided me with turned out to be some of my own personal favourite parts of this book.

The point of telling you much of what I just have is that I want you, the reader, to have a rounded knowledge of the journey I went on while writing this book. Not just the physical journey to Detroit, but the hours I had to spend seeking out these guys. The hundreds upon thousands of emails I had to send to their various acquaintances in order to get anywhere close to them. For a while it seemed hopeless, but I kept on hunting.

I'm not after a round of applause, and certainly not sympathy. This is, after all, my job as the writer and researcher. But to know the experiences that led to the book is to better understand the book and the story.

In a very real way, The Stooges shaped my life. Their very existence caused many of bands to form that I later loved, but even that doesn't reach the crux of it. When I wrote my first book about the MC5, I thought I'd discovered the origins of the music that I would love during my college years. Whether it be Guns N' Roses, Nirvana, Skid Row or even the Ramones, the MC5 seemed to cover all bases.

Then I heard The Stooges for the first time. When I heard this band of social mavericks and the music that they made together, I felt true grit. I felt like I'd just read the first testament for the first time. I felt like I'd been exposed to something truly special without requesting the honour. I was already familiar with Iggy Pop, of course, through tunes like 'Lust For Life' and 'The Passenger' and the movie *Trainspotting*. I knew the name Iggy Pop before I'd ever heard his music, so far had his notoriety spread. But with The Stooges, I was introduced to the musicianship of Ron and Scott Asheton and their playing appealed to me from the very first time I heard '1969' and 'I Wanna Be Your Dog'. I also admired James Williamson's playing on the *Raw Power* album, a style which saw The Stooges come up with a far more traditional set of rock 'n' roll tunes. But the feel of Ron's guitar playing, the sheer monstrosity of the groove, plus Scott's never say die attitude on the drums, really struck a chord with me. I got it from the first time I heard them, and I love it to this day.

The Stooges, like the MC5, influenced hundreds if not thousands of bands that followed in their wake, but unlike the 5, they did so with a completely unconventional approach to rock music. They tore up the rule book, and created something completely fresh, though simultaneously grimy. They're the archetypal punk rock band, and their like will never be seen again. Thank God they're still around.

CHAPTER 1

If the MC5 were Detroit's political spokesmen for the disenchanted youth of the 1960s, then The Stooges were the loutish kids, heckling the imposed semi-intellectualism from the back of the famous Motor City venue, the Grande Ballroom. 'Fuck politics, let's party' they would cry; they were performance artists before there was such a thing. They were punks when the term was only being used to refer to the unfortunate fellow deemed worthy of sexual abuse by the big cheese in prison. Initially at least, they could barely play their instruments. The Stooges were a mess, and the majority of people that heard them despised them for it. This was, after all, the era of the virtuoso. Cream and Led Zeppelin were the top rock bands in the world, and yet The Stooges were performing on stage with household appliances masquerading as instruments. It took a long time for the general public to appreciate The Stooges. True, bands like Dinosaur Jr and Primal Scream have been singing their praises for years, but at the time they were just too 'arty' for Joe Public to enjoy. Nowadays, of course, frontman Iggy Pop is a household name and The Stooges have reformed, thrilling some while leaving others cold all over again. They're certainly playing to bigger audiences and making more money than they did in the 1960s, but then that was a very different time…

Ron Asheton was born on the 17th July, 1948 to parents Ronald and Ann. He was followed by brother Scott on the 16th August, 1949. While living in Washington as a child, Ron's great-aunt and uncle – both of whom were former vaudevillian performers – had a huge impact on his young mind. Before long, Ron had taken up the accordion in an attempt to recreate the awe and splendour that surrounded the past lives of his relatives. By the time the family had moved to Iowa, Ron's interest in that instrument had waned, replaced with a love for The Beatles and The Rolling Stones as was so common at the time.

When Ronald prematurely passed away in 1963, Ann took her two sons and daughter Kathy from Davenport Island to Michigan, settling in Ann Arbor. Though Ronald senior had organised a pension, Ann had to make sure there was always enough for four people to live on, so she got herself a job at the local Ramada Inn.

By the time he reached the eleventh grade, Ron dropped out of high school with his friend Dave Alexander and journeyed to England, visiting the haunts of their heroes, including Denmark Street in London and The Cavern in Liverpool. Speaking in the excellent study of Detroit rock 'n' roll, *Grit, Noise and Revolution*, Ron remembered the excitement of two young friends taking a musical journey of exploration in a foreign land. "We thought that if we went there, we'd learn something. It was amazing to be sixteen and to take a train to Liverpool to go to The Cavern. For one dollar in English money, we could go to the afternoon sessions where five local bands would play."

Ron's travelling companion, Dave Alexander, was born 3rd June, 1947. When his family moved within Michigan from Whitmore Lake to Ann Arbor, he attended Pioneer High School with the Asheton brothers. He dropped out of school after 45 minutes of his first day, to win a bet, a move that was sure to make 'Zander' popular with the Ashetons. In order to finance his trip to England with Ron, Dave would sell his motorbike. The friendship between the two was quickly cemented. Speaking in Joe Ambrose's *Gimme Danger: The Story of Iggy Pop*, Ron Asheton said: "That trip to England was a really great thing. That was what totally changed my life. I could never look back again. Y'know, it's like, 'Nope, I'm never gonna go back to school.' I was a good student, even though I was kicked out – the first guy with long hair. Going back was like, 'This sucks. I don't belong here.' After that giant taste of freedom, to go to The Cavern every afternoon … now it's sitting in the classroom, listening to somebody try to teach me something that I don't give a damn about. 'Fuck this!' So that was the brace that was put on my backbone, to have the guts to go out and do the music thing."

Upon their return to Michigan, both Ron and Dave were expelled from school due to the length of their hair, which by now was considered beyond even controversial. Ron formed a band with his brother Scott and Dave, which would be called The Dirty Shames. Playing guitar alongside Ron would be old friend Billy Cheatham. During an interview for *Plan B* magazine, Ron would tell Sonic Youth's Thurston Moore, "We started The Dirty Shame, which was a band that couldn't really play. We knew two songs – 'We'll Take Our Last Walk Tonight' by The Sir Douglas Quintet and 'The Bells Of Rhymney' by The Byrds. We never really played, but we bullshitted our way into pretending we were rock stars because we looked it and dressed it, and got the job."

Speaking to Paul Trynka, former *Mojo* editor and author of *Open Up And Bleed*, Billy Cheatham recalled his time in The Dirty

Shames. "At that time, Ronnie, Scotty, Dave and I were all childhood friends from 13, 14 years old. Then at high school they all dropped out, and I lost touch 'cause I stayed in school. So from that point on it was sort of a wave association, they were off doing different things – at that time Scotty and Dave weren't playing with anyone when Ron was in the Prime Movers [the local blues-based rock 'n' roll band that created a name for themselves around Detroit with their prolific gigging]. Dave started out playing guitar, and Ron was playing bass. Then when the band formed, Ron wanted to play guitar, he was advancing constantly. You have always been able to hear the bass influence in a lot of the guitar leads, and Dave started playing bass."

Cheatham has fond memories of working with Dave Alexander. "He was a great guy, one of those guys you thought you could size up by looking at him then realise later there were so many facets to him. But he was nuts, deep down, just a crazy kid! He was first to experiment with anything that came along; he was the guy that would get booze before reefer. We knew reefer was there, and he had his sights set on it. [He] was ready to go all out. He was very interested in the occult. Had a real spiritual bent to him. I think he was raised catholic, lost interest in conventional Christianity, introduced me to a lot of things, introduced me to Aleister Crowley ... and Madame Blavatskty, he was into her. He also was fascinated by George Harrison, used him as a compass. But he was really into spiritualism."

Cheatham also recalls his early opinions of the Asheton brothers. "We were all outcasts for one reason or another. Ron was heavy ... (not real heavy) for a kid. Then they had the added stigma of being new kids in town ... Ron and I made friends soon after I got here. Scotty and I made friends too. I didn't know they were brothers. I was friends with both of 'em, Ron through a couple of classes we shared. We shared a sense of humor – *Mad* magazine. Scotty and I were friends again on a level of absurdity. I met him playing football. It was really kind of a shock finding out they were brothers. They were different externally. Scott was … bigger, and had a good frame on him … and [the way he] used his eyes, that scowl he gets! I don't think he ever had to fight, never had to fight to prove himself. They weren't intimidated by Ron. He was smaller, came across as more intellectual, a different kind of guy. Once you get to know them, there are so many common threads like with Kathy [Asheton, Ron and Scott's sister], they have a shared sense of humor, I guess from being close when they were growing up. [Iggy] felt he was an outcast 'cause he grew up in a trailer park, he hated that. He probably felt like an outcast. Ronnie, Scotty and I – we were, no doubt about it."

Iggy doesn't remember exactly how he met the brothers. Speaking to the author, he said, "Y'know, I probably don't but in my mind, somehow Ron was involved with a group of people that were kind of called the beatniks in high school, and that was Bill Kirchen who went on to have a solid career as a country/bluegrass artist in the US. There was a fella named Ricky Hickinbottom too. And he was just around the campus. I don't quite remember how I first ran into him. His brother, in my memory was one of a group of three, including Dave Alexander, his brother and their friend Roy. The three of them used to hang around the corner of State Street and Liberty in Ann Arbor, Michigan, in front of Marshall's drug store, just watching people go by and being classic US street corner layabouts. I worked across the street at a record store. That's my memory anyway. Later, pretty early on, I was aware of Ron playing the bass and somehow I'd seen him playing in a cover band called The Chosen Few. I remember Scott asking me if I would show him some stuff on the drums … That's about as much as I remember."

Speaking in his book, *I Need More*, about the Ashetons, Iggy would say that, "These guys were the laziest, delinquent sort of pig slobs ever born. Really spoiled rotten and babied by their mother.

Scotty Asheton – he was a juvenile delinquent. His dad had died, his and Ron's, so they didn't have much discipline at home."

Ronald senior may have passed away early, but his love of the army still had time to rub off on Ron, who would develop an interest in German military memorabilia that would over the years be described varyingly as either unsavoury or harmless.

Bizarrely, The Dirty Shames managed to build up their own reputation by word of mouth to such a degree that they received an offer to open for The Rolling Stones, despite never having played a show in public. Perhaps wisely – and certainly bravely – Ron declined the invitation.

When that first version of a band with Scott and Dave didn't seem to be working out, or at least wasn't working out as fast as he would have liked, Ron joined an already established band called The Prime Movers. He had been recommended to the band by an acquaintance from a local record store that they used to hang out at, Discount Records. The name of the helpful one was Jim Osterberg, aka Iggy Pop.

Very little needs to be added to the masses of words written about the man who would become Iggy Pop; back then, Jim Osterberg would join The Prime Movers from his former charges The Iguanas in a drummer capacity, and because of his association with his former, more 'pop' band, the very serious Prime Movers re-christened him 'Iggy'. The Prime Movers formed in the summer of 1965 and featured the talents of Michael and Dan Erlewine, and pianist Bob Sheff. While speaking with the website I94bar.com, Michael Erlewine recalled Iggy's impact on the group. "Iggy played in a local band that mostly played for fraternities, called the Iguanas. That was how we met one another. Iggy liked what we were doing and soon joined up as our drummer. He came across as a shy, active, and ambitious young man. The band liked Iggy and vice versa. Girls loved him, as he had long hair, long eyelashes, and appeared bashful around them. He loved to look down at the floor, when they crowded around him, and bat his eyelashes. They went wild …

"The Prime Movers was the first hippie-style or new-style band in the Ann Arbor/Detroit area. Along with the MC5, who in the beginning appeared in suits, we helped to mark a change in what bands were. We had been to Chicago and seen the blues greats (like Muddy Waters, Howlin' Wolf, Little Walter, Magic Sam, etc.) play, so we had no real interest in groups like The Rolling Stones, who, like us, used the blues greats as their mentors."

Despite their disaffection with The Rolling Stones, manager Jeep Holland would try to push The Prime Movers towards a 'British Invasion' sound, something that the band resisted fiercely. Michael Erlewine: "We resisted a lot … we tried the suits, but soon abandoned them. We tried going to the teeny hideouts and the teen circuit, but they did not get what we were playing and we did not feel like playing 'Louie, Louie' or whatever they might have liked all night."

Notably, Iggy would eventually be ousted from his drum stool in The Prime Movers by future MC5 master of ceremonies Jessie 'JC' Crawford. Michael Erlewine: "Iggy moved on from us, just like he had from the Iguanas. There was no big fallout that I can remember. Iggy was ambitious and sought to find his way toward the limelight. J.C. Crawford was his replacement and a good drummer and great guy, at that."

Very quickly, Ron realised that he was out of his usual zone playing with The Prime Movers. "They were very serious. I played with the group for a while. That's when I really learned how to play. I dug the blues, but I wanted to play more straight rock 'n' roll."

Iggy Pop: "The Prime Movers were a working campus far-advanced band. I think Ron played with us for a while and got fired for not coming to a rehearsal or something like that. It was my fault that he got in the band. The guys in The Prime Movers were an older crowd and they'd had an older drummer who was named Spider Wynn, and he wasn't really socially cut from the same cloth as the rest of us. They were sort of hippy neo-beats and he was an old school greaser. So they got me and I was about six years too young, and then I brought in my young friend. He didn't last long. He was too easy going for that band."

Ron's time in The Prime Movers came to a fairly abrupt end and then it was Jim who would help him get a job with Scot Richardson's The Chosen Few; while with that band, Ron would have the honour of playing the first note on the first night of the newly opened Grande Ballroom – perhaps the most legendary venue in Detroit's entire music history.

Ron Asheton: "That was a great time for me. We were high school kids and we were making some pretty serious money at weekends, without any bills to pay because we were all still living at home. We had a bus to maintain, but that was all. I enjoyed playing bass with [The Chosen Few]. Not all guitarists can play bass, or at least not the way it's meant to be played. But yeah, that was a fun time. It was also while with The Chosen Few that I first met James Williamson."

James Robert Williamson was born on the 29th October, 1949, in Castroville, Texas, where his father was a doctor. After his mother remarried, he found himself with a stepfather who was in the army. When he hit eighth grade, his family moved him to Detroit. Before long, he had formed The Chosen Few with Scot Richardson, but time spent in a juvenile home would seriously hinder his chances of being taken seriously by his colleagues and friends. James Williamson: "I was incorrigible. Basically, I was kind of stupid, young. I wouldn't do what anybody told me to do. It was an interesting season. I was trying to grow my hair long, and they didn't like that at my school. I thought that Bob Dylan would never cut his hair, and they said you have to, and we didn't agree, so I got sent to 'juvie' and then they buzzed all of my hair off! I guess I found out a little bit about fighting city hall."

Speaking to the author, James Williamson explained: "I started The Chosen Few with Scot Richardson when we were both in high school. We developed the band for a couple of years and then I got into that trouble and I had to go to juvenile home and then I went off to school in New York, so I wasn't with the band anymore. When I came back, Ron had joined by that point and I got a chance to meet him. He was a good bass player. One night up in Ann Arbor, they were playing a fraternity job, which they frequently did and I went up with them, and Iggy was there as well. So I got to meet him at the same time. That's kind of the beginning of getting to know those guys."

The Chosen Few were led by legendary Detroit musician Scot Richardson, who would go on to form the Scot Richardson Case (SRC). *Rusted Chrome*, an on-line guide to Michigan rock 'n' roll, would describe Richardson's Chosen Few as, "one of the original *Hideout* club bands [a venue which, along with Hideout Records, was a collective that helped fuel Detroit's scene in the 1960s] – tho' they were also the first to play on opening night at the Grande – and among the best (maybe even ahead) of their time, Chosen Few was a seminal Detroit outfit which ended up notable more for its contributions to other groups than for their own musical endeavours. They passed their vocalist Scot Richardson along to the Fugitives which, in turn became Scot Richardson Case (SRC) and guitarist Asheton later joined his brother Scott and [Iggy] in forming the Psychedelic Stooges, which eventually included Williamson as well."

Though history may not have remembered The Hideout Club with the same level of prestige as it has The Grande Ballroom, it was The Hideout that provided many of Detroit's future legends with a place to play on a Friday night. Everyone from Bob Seger and Ted Nugent's Amboy Dukes to the MC5 and the Chosen Few passed through the club's doors. The club had been leased by Dave Leone and Punch Andrews with a view to promoting local band

The Fugitives, who would eventually include Scot Richardson in their numbers. Music historian Dick Rosemont wrote in *Michigan Punk Rock*, "Opening night of The Hideout in May of '64 brought 87 people and two fights. But there was this band playing 'Louie Louie' and doing things people had never heard before on stage. The word spread: two weeks later, 337 teenagers showed up."

When a hefty percentage of the teen crowd adopted a hippie stance and subsequently departed to The Grande, the original Harper Woods [a suburb of Detroit] club closed down in 1967. The other [local rock 'n' roll clubs]lasted only a bit longer but The Hideout name lived on as Bob Seger and Punch Andrews' production company."

Former Grande manager Russ Gibb told the author: "I vaguely remember [The Chosen Few]. I was so busy figuring out whether we were gonna have anybody [at the Grande on opening night for The Chosen Few show] and we did – I think we had about 68 people. It was either '86 or '68, I can't remember. But I thought, *At least we're gonna pay the bills for the band*. I can't remember if we gave them $15 or $25. It wasn't very much. I don't remember The Chosen Few specifically. I just remember that we had a band and I was happy with that. My impression was that they were one of the few bands that were out playing gigs. [Their manager] Jeep Holland … was one of the few guys cultivating live bands back then. I met Ron Asheton for the first time, that would have been the first night, but it was very perfunctory. I was trying to get the place going. I remember I had been to a toy store. I had bought a bunch of silly toys. I had a play box that I thought might be an attraction. We were trying to do things a little bit off the wall. At that time, we had no equipment. They brought their own equipment. I loved the name. Scot Richardson was an amazing kid. He just did so many different things. Of any person, even more than Ron, Richardson's name stood out to me. I do remember the two brothers were both in rock bands, which must have driven the parents crazy. At that time, being in a rock band was a new adventure. A lot of kids weren't down that path yet."

With Richardson now within the wings of a new band, The Fugitives, Ron Asheton found himself facing a dilemma about which act to side with, as David Carson wrote in *Grit, Noise And Revolution*. "Soon, [Iggy] was on the phone to his old buddies Ron and Scott Asheton. After convincing them to come to Chicago and give him a ride back home, Iggy asked if they wanted to form a new band. At the time, The Chosen Few were breaking up, and Ron was faced with a choice of staying with Scot Richardson in a new band backed with money and good equipment, or going with his 'true buds,' brother Scott and Iggy. He chose the latter."

Despite being a bass player with The Chosen Few and The Prime Movers, Ron would switch back to playing guitar with this new band, as he had done with The Dirty Shames, allowing old friend Dave Alexander to come back in on bass. Ron Asheton: "No one could ever play his bass parts like Dave. It weaves its way around the riff and it's great. Dave was our friend already and that's how he got in the band. He was learning his way with the rest of us, but he became a great player. He also had a car, which was a big factor in him getting in the band." The four young men would first rehearse at Ann Asheton's place before moving on to the Alexander's. When they had frustrated and annoyed all of their family members, they rented a house to both live and rehearse in. In order to get the rent paid, Ron would work in a headshop [a store that specialises in selling marijuana-related paraphernalia] and Iggy in a restaurant, waiting tables.

The building they rented was a Victorian student house in the middle of the University of Michigan campus in Forest Court. The students, Ron would tell Iggy Pop biographer Paul Trynka, thought that the future Stooges would be respectful tenants. "But woe betide the day those frat dudes let us in, 'cause we totally destroyed the building."

Iggy Pop thinks the idea of starting a band together with the brothers was his own. "As far as I remember it was me. But it could have been anybody [laughs]. As so many people are at pains to point out, my mind is Swiss cheese. But in my memory it was me. I think half of my motivation was to get that ride home from Chicago, where I was striking out as a blues drummer, badly.

The fact was that right from the get-go when we appeared in person, the guys could play. The two of them. The brothers could play right off. It's just that what they could play wasn't the sort of stuff that you were supposed to be able to play to go by the rules of the nascent American rock industry, and that got everybody really fucking pissed off. But it was what they could play. They couldn't play 'Johnny B. Goode', but they could play something else and as soon as they started, Scott's playing had authority and Ron's playing had wit and an elegance. An elegant touch. He never really put a foot wrong. Dave took a couple of gigs. He was sort of a friend who would operate my strange, invented instruments. But once he picked up the bass, it didn't take him long either to be interesting on it, and I recently heard an old tape from Soldier Field [an infamous 1970 show in Chicago which also featured the MC5 on the bill] and his playing is superb. He was a mercurial personality, and had absolutely no discipline at home, so there were huge lapses possible from him. But all three of these people were intelligent musicians, [and] their intelligence went over the heads of a lot of very ordinary people who were trying really hard to be intelligent. That's what I think.

Ron's always been the kind of person who can sit back and groove all the way through a party without getting really messed up. He's always been that way. Almost kind of a smooth operator. An instigator, on one level. But he has a very conservative side. That's true. Scott shares some of my vulnerabilities. Scott's more a sort of very gifted person who can easily go on a limb. But as far as how we were spending our time, we were all experimenting [with different drugs, depending on which member], and going to party type events, musical events, social events that lasted all night and involved all sorts of people in all sorts of ways. But that was also average. We were part of a subculture in our town that involved hundreds of people. They were pretty average. They weren't the kind of guys that were gonna act out strange shit – that would be more my department. They weren't gonna make a spectacle of themselves. I started that right out of high school when I was still a drummer in The Iguanas, my high school cover band. I started growing my hair and dyed it platinum blonde – I looked like Gorgeous George the wrestler or something. I was only 18 and we got ourselves a summer gig at a teen club where they served Cherry Coke at the bar. I managed to get my first DUI (Driving Under the Influence) and my first mug shot that summer, and got the band fired. Y'know, all that sort of thing, before I ever encountered the other fellas. I was sort of one of those people that was definitely trying to get some attention. I didn't know how much of that was conscious. It's just different strokes for different folks, y'know. Ron and Scott were more laid back about everything.

Y'know, I found Dave difficult as a person. He ... probably had the least confidence in the idea of thing [The Stooges band] in the beginning and that was hard. My toughest job starting the group, or for anyone starting a group and trying to hold it together, is to get everybody to believe that this one unified goal is attainable. He had a problem with that. He was the most difficult one to bring into it. But as he went along, he played better than I realised at the time. I listen back, and it's pure, it's tongue in cheek, and one of the best things about it is that at times he'll improvise using notes that no trained musician would ever use. You wouldn't even hear it on a Miles Davis record. You wouldn't even hear Reggie Workman doing this on a Coltrane record. I'll listen to him and he makes some improvisations at the end of 'No Fun' I think, and I can practically hear his mind thinking as he looks at the fret board 'I think I'll put my fingers over here and try those notes.' You can hear him having fun playing. It has a playfulness and a buoyancy about it, and it's a really good foil for Ron. Ron plays like a sabre, like fencing. Ron's playing has a very fine point and a light touch to it. He's not a heavy musician. Dave managed not to tie that down. To me, he manages to play in such a way that keeps things light, sort of like if Ron was a comedian on a talk show, Dave would be his straight man. The guy that sits there and laughs at his jokes, and keeps the thing moving along. And in fact, that's the way they related to each other socially. They would stay up all night. Ron would suggest television shows to watch and they'd sit there cracking jokes about them. Later, when I became a kind of real life TV show, they'd stay up all night and crack jokes about me. They had a wall of the house that they papered up together with their own sarcastic posters advertising the group, like 'Come see Iggy – see him shit green. See him puke!' etc, etc."

Before all this legendary stage eccentricity plunged him into the spotlight, Iggy has, however, fond memories of writing songs with Ron. "It's like dealing with a rock star, immediately. And it was immediately before he had ten cents in his pocket or a recording to his name. It's like dealing with a rock star, and later I've written with some very big ones and there's just no difference. Basically, he has a genuine, unique talent. His big contribution to the group initially was coming up with these two world-class eternal riffs in 'No Fun' and 'I Wanna Be Your Dog'. He came up with each of those in his own way on his own time – I wasn't part of it. Personally I believed that, because he smoked so much marijuana and the whole thing was so new to him, that he wasn't gonna take them any further. I took it upon myself to suggest some chord changes and breaks for the songs, and slight variations ... We usually worked separate like that. In other words, he'd have an idea,

I'd hear it and I'd take it away, or I'd have an idea and he'd play it in a completely different way that took it to a place I never could have done.

For instance, with 'Fun House' all I really had was the concept of a drone. I thought I had a bass riff, although Ron tells me that Dave came up with that and that's possible too. But what really makes the swing is the counterpart – the groove that Ron and Steve get into. We did very, very little sitting down. We wrote a few things like that – 'Not Right', 'TV Eye' was done that way, 'Real Cool Time', but the main thing was the reaction from me. I'd get very excited when I heard this guy play something that just sounded great. I thought, *Once again he's not putting a foot wrong*. He never played *anything* that made me wince."

The time spent in Forest Court seems, by all accounts, to have been split between rehearsing and behaving like, as Kathy Asheton [their sister] would word it, "crazed, pig-style, crazed bachelors, fun times." By early 1968, however, the new band was playing live. The group's name came from their favourite TV show – Ron would stay up for most of the evening watching late night TV shows and his own favourite was *The Three Stooges*, and during the summer of '67, he realised that, "we're like The Stooges, but we're psychedelic. Let's call ourselves The Psychedelic Stooges." That overlong moniker would stick for some time, but most people were referring to them as simply 'The Stooges' long before they officially dropped the 'Psychedelic'.

In Clinton Heylin's book, *From The Velvets To The Voidoids*, Ron Asheton poetically described their early shows thus: "Usually we got up there and jammed one riff and built into an energy freak-out, until finally we'd broken a guitar or one of my hands would be twice as big as the other and my guitar would be covered in blood."

Speaking to the author, Iggy Pop: "We weren't interested in anything like writing a song or making a chord change. I didn't bother with anything like that until I had a recording [contract]; once I had the contract I thought I'd better really learn how to write some songs – so I did. Our [early] music was flowing and very conceptual. We'd have just one given song, called 'Wind Up', or I'd change the title to 'Asthma Attack' or 'Goodbye Bozos', or, I don't know, 'Jesus Loves The Stooges'. So, la-de-da, that's how we started out."

Though Iggy was originally intended to be the drummer, it was a performance by The Doors – and particularly Jim Morrison – at the University Of Michigan, that made Ron realise that they already had a similarly charismatic frontman within their ranks, recognising Iggy's "need to perform more freely." At that show, Morrison deliberately antagonised the crowd by singing in a high-pitched, Betty Boop style voice. Jim Osterberg was suitably impressed. Sort of. He remembers thinking during the show, "Look at how awful they are, and they've got the number one single in the country! If this guy can do it, so can I."

Billy Cheatham would tell Paul Trynka of his on-going relationship with The Stooges, and the Ashetons in particular. "Jim wanted to be the lead performer, started putting it together, then right about that time I left the state; they had formed the band, and were living out on Vreeland Rd. I went to a couple of jobs with them there as a visiting friend. Then I left town again … [and when I came back] they were living on Forest Court, and Jim wrote some pretty good songs down there. When I finally got back, I was literally just passing through, had stopped to see my parents, was on my way to Boston, and [Jim] said, "Why don't you work for us, be a road guy in the summer?" I thought *Cool* – I don't have to look for a job. And I stayed. I think it was June 1969. I was friends with the band and lived there at the hall, we hung around together. As you looked at the house, I was living in the front room, right off the practice room, which had been the living room. Dave Alexander lived right on the other side of me. Ronnie lived on the first floor too at that point. We had a TV room, and Ron was on the back corner. Scott lived on the second floor and Jim lived in the attic, had the whole first floor."

MC5 manager and legendary Detroit beatnik and political activist John Sinclair has his own early memories of the Ashetons. "I didn't know who they were at that time. I knew all of those guys quite well later, but I came out of the beatnik/jazz scene and I liked the MC5 because they played 'Black To Comm'. I got to like the rest of them, but that was later. I didn't know Ron as a person until the 1970s, but I knew him as a Stooge. To me, they were these little weird guys … I knew Iggy a little bit because of The Prime Movers, the band he was in with Michael Erlewine."

Ron Asheton recalled in *Gimme Danger* the band's early experimentation with music. "It did start out with Iggy getting a Farfisa organ, my brother coming up, using timbales and a snare drum and the 50-gallon oil drums. I would use the bass guitar that I was playing with fuzztone and wah-wah pedal. We invented instruments: putting a contact mike on the 50-gallon oil drum; putting a mike against the lip of a blender with water; taking a washboard, putting a contact mike on it, and Iggy getting up on it with golf shoes with spikes and kinda doing rhythm things. We found that if you took a microphone and put it on the bass drum mike stand, take a funnel and you can lift it up and down and make different kinds of … almost like a bass synthesiser or something. Whirrrrr … just different weird feedback through the PA. Or taking an old Kustom amp and crashing it, putting the reverb unit on high … 'Gee it sounds like a thunderstorm or a rainstorm.' We got Dave Alexander to do that, and that's what he used to do … work all the weird instruments while Iggy played keyboards and I played the bass and my brother played this kinda bizarre drum set."

The MC5's Michael Davis told the author of his early impressions of The Stooges: "On the first night that they played the

Grande Ballroom as The Psychedelic Stooges, what comes to mind was that Iggy had painted his face silver. That was very attention-getting and radical. It wasn't like the rock 'n' roll vibe that we were trying to display. It wasn't like that; it was more like the carnival, like the clowns. I remember watching the band play, and being pretty unimpressed by the music. It was like their first show, and they were pretty poised for their first show, but on a scale of 1–10, they were about a three. I thought they were gutsy, they were definitely unique and they weren't trying to be like anybody else, but they were pretty limited as far as what they were offering. Except for the singer, who was beyond normal rock 'n' roll convention. We as a group accepted them, just on the sheer fact that they had a lot of balls to be doing that."

When recalling his first meeting with Dave Alexander, Davis couldn't help but chuckle during our interview. "Dave Alexander was *so* shy … he would barely speak to you, and if he would speak to you, you'd have to ask him a question and he'd speak to you from like behind a mask. He was the most introverted person I've ever met in rock 'n' roll. I think the only person he ever really talked to was Ron. Any time I was ever in his presence, he had literally nothing to say."

By now, Iggy had taken to calling Ron, Scott, Dave and Billy Cheatham the 'Dum Dum boys'. Mike Davis: "I always thought that was kind of a condescending thing to say. I call him Iggy, by the way. I don't call him Jim, like everybody that seems to be so chummy with him. I call him Iggy and if he wanted to be called Jim, he'd tell me. I didn't think Iggy was justified in being so … harsh. I know that it was kind of a tongue-in-cheek thing and he was actually putting himself down [but] it just seemed a little poorly placed."

Mike Davis is adamant that there was no competitive edge between the MC5 and their baby brother band. "There was no rivalry because we thought they were kind of like junior high school. We were the big shots and The Stooges were just learning.

They were the apprentice band. We wouldn't be so coarse as to acknowledge that there was a rivalry … we'd hang out at their house, sit on the couch and play records. We'd have a turntable, stacks of albums and people would congregate at the house, somebody would take over the turntable and start playing jams. The volume levels were never a problem [and] there was a spirit that was so cool. I don't know if people do that nowadays. We'd drink beer, smoke hash, girls would come over and the bands would hang out. It was very lively and spirited. Their place was always fun to go to because it was very undemanding. You could just go and hang out, and the vibe was always good."

John Sinclair told the author: "I saw them live for the first time when they played at Ron Richardson's house [The Stooges' first manager]. My mind was totally blown. It was when you saw them on stage that you saw what it really was, but here they were in a living room with a vacuum cleaner. There wasn't any dancing around. When I saw them on stage for the first time, I said 'That's the greatest shit I've seen since the MC5.' And they weren't anything like that, they were totally unique. That's what I liked about them. It was like seeing an [experimental artist] Laurie Anderson show, and then a rock 'n' roll gig, y'know? Iggy had shaped the music so that it didn't matter that they couldn't play too well. Scott would pound out a rhythm, Ron and Dave would play something that would drone. They only had 20 minutes, and they didn't have any tunes. They would just make the whole thing up. The whole thing was crafted out of an idea of what it was, a concept. It was brilliant."

Russ Gibb: "To me, John Sinclair was the one that brought The Stooges to my attention. Iggy was an amazing character onstage. He was like a marionette, self-propelled. He's still like that, too. The first time I came across him, he came with a Reynolds wrap suit. An aluminium suit, the stuff you use to wrap packages. Someone had wrapped him up in this thing, and on stage he looked a little like the tin man in *The Wizard Of Oz*. He slowly stripped it off during the performance. The Grande was famous for the closeness between the audience and the stage. You could touch the performers. I remember one time, I saw Iggy jumping off the stage into the audience. My concern was lawsuits. *Oh my God, what if this kid breaks his neck. Or if he hurts one of our customers, we're out of business.* I remember talking, I think to John, about the stage dives. I was assured Iggy knew what he was doing. As far as I know, Iggy was the first one to stage dive. Later on, I saw it a lot at another club I had called the Greystone, which was my punk club. I saw lots of kids climb up on stage and stage dive. He may go down in history as the originator of stage diving. He may be given an award sometime, or a plaque. 'The founder of stage diving.'"

The frontman went much further than that. The self-mutilation was something that was very, very weird," continues Russ Gibb. "Afterwards, I saw more of it. In private though, Iggy's a quiet person. Nowadays, he looks a lot like his father. His father and I taught together. The kids at high school in Dearborn called him Iggy's pop. There are people to this day who don't think he was a great musician, but he's certainly a great showman ... Most kids were brought up on television, and they had never seen the circus. They'd never seen a vaudeville show, which I had. They'd never seen a real magician's show ... Iggy was into that mould of a real showman. Kids had not had that, and it was exciting to see them react. Iggy fitted in perfect. He was all over the stage. He was like a mad marionette. The focus definitely was Iggy. I don't think the average kid could tell you who was in Iggy's band. That's a shame though, because the music quality wasn't due to Iggy. I was interested in the showmanship, and of course the number of people that would buzz about a band. You gotta remember, I was a business guy."

Ron Asheton: "Russ Gibb was going to be our manager. He took us to see The Doors. I have fond memories of Russ, and him letting us play at The Grande. We played there at least once or twice a month."

David Carson would write about an infamous early Stooges show in his book, *Grit, Noise And Revlution*, which "came about after booking agent Jeep Holland convinced the owner of a Romeo, Michigan, club called Mother's to book the still unknown band in August 1968. Iggy arrived wearing a pair of skin-tight brown vinyl pants. During their performance, Iggy's crotch split open, momentarily exposing the singer's personal property. The brief incident would have probably been forgotten except for the fact that a girl in the audience happened to be the daughter of a state police trooper stationed nearby. Later, as Iggy sat backstage with a towel wrapped around him, state troopers came bursting through the front door, one yelling: 'Where's that Iggy!'"

Thanks to that early bit of drama, Iggy's parents had to take their son to court, where he would receive a $40 fine for disorderly conduct. If a sign was needed as to the chaos that would follow the band around for the remainder of their careers, this was it.

Speaking in *Gimme Danger*, MC5's Wayne Kramer remembers the first time he saw The Stooges live. "Iggy was sitting on the floor and he had a steel guitar with some kind of modal tuning and he was bashing away on it. He had this vacuum cleaner too. He held it in front of the mike and made different noises with it. The whole thing was tremendously abstract and avant-garde. People didn't know what to make of it. They didn't know to laugh and they didn't know to take it serious."

The Stooges' first manager was Ron Richardson, who would be rechristened The Mad Professor by Grandma Asheton due to his tendency to tinker with gadgets. While he and the band were living in Vreeland Street, their shared farmhouse on Vreeland Road, he glued egg boxes to the wall in an attempt to create soundproofing and stem the tide of complaints from the neighbours.

Ron Richardson remembers in *Gimme Danger* that, "I was managing The Stooges and teaching school at the same time. It was just like being in debt and deeper in debt. There were promises from various promoters, but it was not happening as fast as you think it should happen. Then we went our separate ways."

Management responsibilities for The Stooges then fell at the feet of Jimmy Silver, a friend of John Sinclair. "Jimmy Silver and I were very close friends. He was a very 'Sixties' kind of guy, a rock 'n' roll hippie intellectual like myself. I guess the way Jimmy got involved was that I was looking after the MC5, my brother worked for [legendary Detroit rock 'n' roll band] The Up. We were all in the same social circle." Inevitably, with such eccentric and highly charged live shows, and with the MC5 attracting record label interest to the Detroit area, it wasn't long before The Stooges started getting approached by 'the biz'.

In a similar fashion to that of the MC5, the lives of The Stooges were changed forever by the visit of Elektra Records' A&R man, Danny Fields. He was in town to see the 5 and was already suitably impressed with them when Wayne Kramer very decently said to Fields, "If you like us, you'll love our baby brother band." After watching both bands live, Fields got on the phone to Elektra head honcho Jac Holzman, who instructed him to offer the MC5 $20,000 and The Stooges $5,000. Both managers leapt at the offer.

Though his official title at Elektra was 'Publicity Director'. When Iggy met him after the show that would eventually lead to The Stooges getting signed, he was unimpressed. "I was playing a free gig, one of my few. It got to the end of our show, I was just letting the amps play and shooed the band off. So I was just wandering around. I had this maternity dress and a white face and I was doing unattractive things, spitting on people, things like that … I wander off the stage and this guy says, 'You're a star!' Just like in the movies. I believed he was an office boy who just wanted to meet me and impress me. He didn't look like what I thought a record company executive should look like. He was dressed like us, in jeans and a leather jacket."

In the sleeve notes to the Stooges' eventual debut album, Fields says, "When Iggy came off the stage, I went over to him, gushing about the show, telling him I was from Elektra Records and was eager to get them a contract. 'Speak to my manager', he said, still walking toward the dressing room, not even looking at me."

Billy Cheatham remembers his own opinions of Fields. "I liked him a lot, I wasn't that close, but he was a nice guy. I know he had that relationship with Jim. If I can remember one big thing about the whole time, it seemed things were predicated on Jim's relationship with whoever was around. Dan and Jim got along … Jim was the centre of the solar system in that sense."

The MC5's Michael Davis was delighted to see The Stooges getting a deal at the same time 'as his own band. "I was very happy about that. By that time, they were building a pretty big local following. There was definitely a Stooges camp of fans. This was right in line with all of the psychedelic music, people getting wasted. They created a fan base that was different from the MC5. Stooge-ville has no room for social criticism. They had more to do with satire. There was more camaraderie than rivalry. What they were about was very artful. Those guys were going at it with humour. They were about laughing. When they got signed to Elektra, I thought it was great because they deserved it. It wasn't about them being great musicians, it was about the fact that they were presenting a show that was deeper than what was on the surface. This subliminal message was working."

John Sinclair: "The signing took place a couple of days later. But to us, the signing was when they said that they were gonna sign us. That was when we felt signed."

Very much out of the blue, Iggy celebrated his new record deal by getting married to Wendy Weisberg about a month later. Ron advised Iggy not to marry Weisberg, but he did enjoy the wedding.

"I wore my Luftwaffe fighter's jacket, with a white shirt, with a Nazi Knight's Cross with oak leaves and swords. On the jacket, I had my Iron Cross first class, the ribbon bars, the Russian front Iron Cross second class, and my riding boots and jodhpurs. I was the best man. Our manager, Jimmy Silver, who is Jewish, was the minister."

Silver did indeed conduct the service, having been ordained by the Universal Life Church (such is the nature of that particular organization, they even offer 'free online ordinations' today, something that the author couldn't resist while conducting research for this book. The Reverend Brett Callwood at your service).

Billy Cheatham: "Dave Alexander and I went and bought new tennis shoes for the wedding. I remember going through the line and Dave saying, 'Bet you these tennis shoes last longer than Iggy's marriage.'" Sadly, Alexander's prophecy would prove to be true. A month after the big day, Weisberg was gone.

Friend of the band and singer with The Cult Heroes, Hiawatha Bailey, recalled his first Stooges experience to the author: "Here in Ann Arbor, there's 'the diag' which is central campus. Back then, we'd be walking around campus tripping on many more than needed hits of clinical LSD and stuff, years before that stuff was put on the controlled substances list in this country. There was this crew of guys that I had never seen the likes of before. They'd be cruising like a gang of rebels. Four in total, wearing skin-tight black leather and led by this dude, this shirtless, bellbottom-wearing dude. It turns out that that was The Stooges. I started hanging out with John Sinclair and the people at the White Panther house [the idealist political group set up by Sinclair and associated with the MC5], then I started hauling equipment for The Up. We would all go to The Grande Ballroom, then we'd come back to town and go to this place called Fifth directly across from the diag. It was an all night coffee shop/restaurant/hang-out where everybody that was from Ann Arbor would go down to

Detroit to play and hang out. Late night, The Stooges would always be hanging out over there. The first thing that Scott ever said to me, when I was doing something scandalous one night, was 'OK, where are the drugs at? You are the most suspicious person I've ever seen in my life, I know you know where the drugs are.' That freaked me out and I took off! That was my first meeting with 'The Grim Beater', which is what he later became known as.

The Stooges lived in Stooge Manor [The Fun House]. Well, there were lots of times where the guys had equipment and needed to borrow our van (we were fully equipped with our own van). There were lots of times when Iggy would need help and he would call me and ask me to go over to Stooge Manor and pick up certain pieces of equipment. I was in awe of those guys. Back then, I was totally intimidated by those guys. There was The Up and the MC5, and that was the more intellectual crowd. Their audience was into complicated chord progressions and all that stuff. Then there was Scott Morgan and The Rationals, which was more like R&B stuff, like soul. Then there was The Stooges. There were three communes in town, and those that would support The Stooges were always the wildest. Wherever we went, havoc was soon to follow. I fell in real quick with their group of people, with Scott and Ronnie.

There was a show at the Michigan Palace that sticks out. I would just not be myself if I missed a Stooges concert – things would just not go right. I had borrowed this friend of mine's Mustang which didn't even have a license plate on it. I made it down to the concert just in time but couldn't buy a ticket to get in. I took a piece of paper, wrote PRESS on it and stuck it in my hat. There was this chick outside who was crying because she couldn't get in and I said 'Grab hold of my belt loop.' She grabbed the back of my bell-bottoms and we went flying in. I made it all the way to the front, shouting 'press, press, press!' I stopped to buy something for Iggy, because people were always throwing things at those guys. I took this bag of pot. [A man called] Big John pulled me onstage. I ran side stage and wound up and ended up performing at that gig.

There was another time they were supposed to open up at the Dancing Dome, out by an air force base. [Some of] the band had started doing heroin at that point – it was really a low point. The Up were opening for The Stooges, and everybody was starting to throw things at the stage … there weren't that many black dudes around back then and shit, so I went out to the parking lot and there were the guys. They were sitting out on their manager's big black car, Od-ing and shit, while people started to riot and demand that they play.

Another crazy concert was the Funny Farm in Wayne, MI, over on Michigan Avenue. This old hillbilly and his wife had the idea to buy every bar along Michigan Avenue, and they started with this place called The Melody Theatre which was a dirty book store at the front and a dirty movie theatre on the inside – he started doing concerts there. Then he moved down the street and bought the Michigan Palace. In between the Melody and the Michigan Palace was this place that he bought for his son called The Funny Farm. I remember The Stooges played there one night, and they had hired this motorcycle gang to do security. Iggy wound up crawling off stage that night, and he kissed this biker for some stupid reason. The biker had a lead filled glove on and he proceeded to knock Iggy straight out. Iggy lay there twitching for a while."

Bailey also remembers getting on well with Ronnie Asheton but being close friends with Scott. "Ronnie and I are both Cancerians. My birthday is on the 15th and his is two days after that. Ron is not [necessarily] the kind of guy you can just easily get along with, but I do get along with him. It just took a while. A lot of people were intimidated because of the political things I was involved in with The White Panther Party. The Stooges were not that politically oriented. They were just a band that was just playing. We used a band as a speaking organ to carry our politics forward, to get people to sign petitions and to get organised around the world. We had 67 chapters to help us do the things we needed to get done and shit.

Scott has always been my boy. He's really funny. Ron keeps himself to himself, and still now before he goes onstage he's really nervous. Rock [Scott] is just Rock. He's always there, always fun. Ron will tell stories forever, but Rock is usually the root of the stories. Rock is a party animal and Ron had always been distant. Ron was just very fragile, he was reticent to approach people. Dave [Alexander] was great. Dave was pretty cool."

Niagara from Destroy All Monsters [singer in the later band that would feature Ron Asheton, who at the time would be her boyfriend]: "Around September, [The Stooges] started unravelling their clothes in the basement because they had no clothes. Ronnie stopped washing dishes – there was cat shit and filth everywhere and they all moved out. Dave Alexander packed up his suitcase. He takes it, runs down the stairs, and there was this gorgeous stained glass window at the bottom. The suitcase went right through it. It was like a Three Stooges thing. Ronnie's stories always end up like The Three Stooges. Ronnie used to doodle over the TV guide. His mother, Ann, would yell at him for it and rip them up, but I thought they were brilliant. I managed to keep a few, and I had them framed."

A veteran of the Ann Arbor community, Mique Craig was a friend of The Stooges in their formative years and beyond. "The Stooges did one of their very first gigs for a party for me at a nightclub. Recently, I was at an art show and I saw a picture of Scott wearing a red coat, jeans and he had one of my t-shirts on – Mique's party with The Stooges. That was way back.

I remember many nights hanging out with Ronnie and Scott – of course, we were partiers then. We used to do a little bit of everything. We'd stay up all night talking. Ronnie is a Three Stooges addict. We'd stay up and watch The Three Stooges all night, drinking and ... Scotty and I would stay up all night many times, just talking. Scotty is an avid fisherman. Avon have a product called Skin So Soft, and Scott told me that it's the best stuff. He's a big tough guy, and he told me that he puts it all over him when he's fishing to keep the mosquitoes away. Everyone uses it now, but he was one of the first men I heard of using it. Scott wouldn't have just told anybody that.

The guys used to come over and baby-sit my daughter. We'd buy them booze and stuff. Scott and Ronnie's sister Kathy lived with me at the time. We'd go out and leave them there, and they would do Three Stooges acts for her all night. She just loved that."

Stooge Manor – that place was a dump. This old, old, old farmhouse, which was torn down. They finally were evicted – I don't even know if they had any legal means to be in there. It was ratty – you wouldn't believe it. [Iggy] took me up to his room one night, which was in the attic. There was no dry wall or anything. There was this old iron bed with a mattress and a pillow. No sheets, no blankets. The walls were bare and there was a pink ribbon hanging on the wall. He said, 'I put that up there for you, because I thought it'd make it look nicer in here.'"

CHAPTER 2

In June 1969, The Stooges travelled to New York City and spent two days recording their eponymous debut album at The Hit Factory studio, with John Cale taking on the production duties. Cale was already a legend in his own right and was well known to the band for his work with fellow punk pioneers The Velvet Underground. By 1969, Cale had already played bass, electric viola and piano on the classic *The Velvet Underground & Nico* album, aka The Banana Album aka The Andy Warhol Album – and the band had followed that up with the not so impressive but equally notorious *White Light/White Heat* record.

John Davies Cale was born on 9th March, 1942 in the Welsh village of Garnant in the industrial Amman Valley. After discovering his talent for the piano, he studied at Goldsmiths College and the University of London, before settling in New York City. It was here that he hooked up with Lou Reed and the newly formed Velvets. By 1968, Cale and Reed had grown apart and Cale left the band. Enter The Stooges.

Cale may have leapt at the opportunity to produce The Stooges but his opinion of their big brother band was entirely different. "I *hated* the MC5! Heartily! Not because they were conventional rock 'n' roll but because of the violence."

Speaking in *Open Up And Bleed*, Cale explained that when he arrived at the Fun House to hang out with his new charges, he discovered that the fridge was full of beer but contained absolutely no food. "I said, 'What do you fuckin' eat?' and Iggy said, 'Whatever, you know.'"

Ron Asheton: "He'd become a staff producer for Elektra Records, and his first project was us. We felt comfortable because we admired that band, The Velvet Underground. We didn't know any of them personally. I think Iggy had seen them play. I'd never seen them play but we had the records. So I thought, *That's cool. It's somebody different*. He knew his way around the studio because they recorded and he's done a lot of music. I'd never been in a studio, neither had Dave, neither had Scotty. Iggy had been in a studio somewhat, but it was, not overwhelming, but 'Wow'. You're a kid but you're ballsy. You're not afraid, you just wanna get in there and do your thing. So it was cool. We bought our stacks, our big Marshall stacks. The only problem we had was that we didn't realise that normal procedure in a studio isn't to have a Marshall stack turned on 10. It was a very small place, just a rectangle, and it just had some things to block the sound. We were just set up, with me next to the bass in this tiny room. John couldn't really get around the fact that we were gonna do that. He was like, 'Wait a minute, this isn't how it's done. You use little amps, like the old blues guys.' We were like, 'No man, this is how we play.' We need that volume. I get off on that volume. I'm not a guy that's really accomplished on my instrument to the point where I can sit and noodle quietly and whatever. That's our sound, that's what we are.

That power, that big noise. He was going, 'No way.' So we said, 'No way.' So we wound up kind of having a sit down strike, and after a while we compromised so that the amps were on nine instead of ten! That's how we played, that's what we wanted. We just did our own thing. He went with Jac Holtzman and mixed it. He didn't come in and say, 'Hey, boys, you've gotta do this', which was good. He just let us do our own thing. He didn't come in and tell us what to do. Once we got rolling, he just did his thing. Probably the thing he did which I enjoy the most – which was really cool and we didn't expect – was he played viola on 'We Will Fall'. That was really cool. That was, to me, the little teardrop on top of a sad song. I thought that was really cool. Even my brother has mentioned before that he thought it was really cool."

With Cale behind the desk, further Velvet Underground connections were made when Iggy began a turbulent relationship with Nico, the Warhol protégé who had sung on the first Velvets record. The album was complete in two days. Cale actually stated beforehand that they needed to "make the record, forget about what's on stage." For that reason, early Stooges live favourites like 'I'm Sick', 'Asthma Attack', 'Goodbye Bozos' and 'Dance Of The Romance' were given the chop in favour of more 'tuneful' numbers.

The false start at the beginning of album-opener '1969' is typical Stooges humour, but when the famous riff does kick in, it kicks *hard*. Galloping along, it's a tremendous performance from Ron.

'I Wanna Be Your Dog' is next, perhaps still The Stooges' best known song (to the point that the reformed Stooges even play it twice on stage post-2006). This is the sound of Iggy singing with his dick and the rest of the band following his lead. Scott's drums are tribal and fittingly simplistic and Dave's bass chugs along nicely. While Iggy howls away and sings with his libido, it's Ron who once again steals the show, pulling out a sexier riff than had ever been heard at that point. Decadent, raunchy and beautifully feedback-lead, this was a career defining performance from Ron.

'We Will Fall' is an altogether different piece of work. Featuring the viola talents of John Cale, the song has a Buddhist chant quality to it (based, as it is, on a chant by Indian guru Swami Ramdas), and at just over ten minutes long, it certainly isn't easy listening. Still, there's something disturbingly hypnotic about the song, and if it pissed off the masses with it's "Oh gi ran ja ran ja ja ran" chant, then all the better as far as the band were concerned.

'No Fun' is the band at their combatant best. The fact that the Sex Pistols would later adopt the song as their own is a testament to just how well The Stooges captured the general feeling among young people during the late 1960s and 1970s. Again, Ron's repetitive riff is prominent on a song that is basically a scuzzed version of the many 1950s rock 'n' roll classics that littered the radio.

'Real Cool Time' features Ron riffing away seemingly of his own accord while Iggy basically repeats the phrase "We will have a real cool time … tonight" over and over. The song builds and builds, increasing in speed, until it reaches its chaotic finale.

'Ann' is the closest The Stooges ever came to a ballad. Opinions are divided about whether it was inspired by Ann Asheton, or Anne Opie Weher, a regular on the Ann Arbor arts scene. Weher had lost a leg during a battle with cancer and Iggy had taken a liking to her. Still, the spelling of the name in the title implies that Ma Asheton could well be the recipient of the honour. If the song is about Ann Asheton, then Ron and Scott may well have had words with their frontman. Nobody wants to be onstage hearing their friend sing of their mother "You made me shiver with a real thrill" or "Ann, my Ann, I love you Ann."

'Not Right' is another typical Stooges drone. While Ron chops away at his guitar, Iggy sings of how he can't attend to his girl's needs because he's "not right". It may borrow the basic chords from 'I Wanna Be Your Dog' and simply turn them around, but it does it so effectively that it barely matters. The Stooges never were technical geniuses, but they knew how to make a drone sound exciting. 'Not Right' is no different.

The closing song on the record, 'Little Doll', features a bass line apparently borrowed from the song 'Upper And Lower Egypt' by Pharaoh Sanders, but again it doesn't matter. The lyrics are beyond simplistic as Iggy sings to the "prettiest thing I've ever seen." But again, it matters little. This is The Stooges ending on as high a note as they were capable of. The lyrics are positive and fairly romantic for a bunch of apparently disaffected youths, and yet they retain the repetitive, droning quality that lurches through the album, giving the entire record a deconstructed feel and making it so damned exciting. This was an album unlike anything people had heard before. For all that it begged and borrowed from their contemporaries, they had evolved, or more accurately, devolved, the music to such a degree that it brought forward a ragged and under-produced sound that other 'real' musicians would sneer at. Kids feeling equally as under-valued by society in both the USA and the UK would grab onto The Stooges though, and a new form of music would be born.

Mike Davis: "I was amazed by how well they pulled it off. 'No Fun' in particular, I always loved to hear at the Grande. When they played it there, it was more like a chant. When it came out on the record, it had definite choruses and verses and it had song structure. When they played that song at the Grande, it was the two chords back and forth. It was more like a chant – 'no fun, my baby, no fun. No fun, my baby, no fun', again and again … of course, I could have just been trashed! I was a little bit disappointed by that, but overall, the way they performed and the sound of the record was fantastic. I was amazed by how simple and precise everything was, and it worked. I was a little bit amazed by Dave Alexander's bass parts. There's a bit in 'I Wanna Be Your Dog' where he plays two or three notes that are a departure from the bass line. I was in awe of how simple it was and how well it worked." Russ Gibb:

"Did I like the album? Not really. To this day, I still don't think that any album did Iggy justice."

With the album complete, it was time to garner the all-important critics' reviews. Reviewing the album for *Rolling Stone*, Edmund O. Ward said, "The Stooges, formerly the Psychedelic Stooges, hail from Ann Arbor, Michigan, where, in case you've never been told, they do things high-powered – high-powered music, high-powered doping, high-powered fucking, high-powered hyping. The Stooges used to share a house with another local band whom they greatly resemble – the MC5. The picture on the cover of the album shows the Stooges to be four nice middle-class kids gone wrong wearing brand new synthetic leather jackets and pouting at the camera in a kind of snot-nosed defiance. They don't look at all that bright, although they may be college dropouts, and I'm sure that all the high school kids in the area dig the hell out of them. Three of them play guitar, bass, and drums, while picturesque Iggy sings in a blatantly poor imitation of early Jagger style. The instrumentalists sound like they've been playing their axes for two months and playing together for one month at most, and they just *love* wah-wah and fuzz just like most rank amateur groups. The lyrics are sub-literate, as might be inferred by the title …

So, cats and kitties, if you want to have a real cool time, just bop on down to you local platter vendor and pick up the Stooges' record, keeping in mind, of course, that it's loud, boring, tasteless, unimaginative, childish, obnoxious…."

Ward pretty much hit the nail on the head, as John Sinclair will attest. "I loved it. I still love it. When I hear 'I Wanna Be Your Dog', I get excited. It's 1969, OK. Those are great performances. If they were gonna make a record for Elektra, they were gonna have to have some tunes together."

Creem magazine got a little closer to the truth when they said this of Ron's guitar playing on the record: "The dangerous [band] manage to quickly get down to the nitty-gritty of sensual frustration for all the neo-American adolescent malehood … '1969' is the perfect expression of the oldest complaint of rebellious anarcho/crazy youth. Iggy sounds a lot younger than 22 for the horny American youth whose fantasies he summarises. 'I Wanna Be Your Dog' is reminiscent of early Velvet Underground music carrying it into even more bizarre levels. 'No Fun' features some physically abusive guitar playing by Ron Asheton. Throughout the album, Asheton reveals himself as an insane master of the power The Stooges channel into their music. This is probably the guitar style of the future."

Not a bad prediction as it goes, as before long guitar players across the globe would be latching on to Ron Asheton and his style. It was also incredibly intuitive of the writer to note that this was as much Ron Asheton's record as it was Iggy's. On stage, it's justifiable to say that Iggy stole the show. It was his theatrics that got people watching and, ultimately, listening. But on record, when the audience had nothing to look at but the four dour faces adorning the sleeve, Asheton came into his own.

Almost comically, the debut album would eventually be released in August 1969, during the same week as the first Woodstock Festival. It wasn't only *Creem* and *Rolling Stone* who were complimentary either, with *Circus* coming out and saying that, "Nobody ever claimed they were superb musicians, especially they; they just do it as best they know how, not caring much about criticism and less about the people not equipped to dig what they're doing. The album is long and rangey, musically average, but emotionally as intense as, well … why don't you supply the analogy?"

Reporting for *Fusion* magazine, future Patti Smith guitarist Lenny Kaye said of the album that, "By any formal criteria, they are a retrogressive group, a pale copy of the early Rolling Stones. Their music revolves around one modified Bo Diddley chord progression, and neither the singing nor musicianship on their album attains any memorable level of competence ... The world of the Stooges, simply, revolves around boredom. Not only a mere lack of something to do, but rather a total negation of *anything* to do. The Stones used to touch on this feeling when they sang 'I can't get no satisfaction', but the meaning of their song was set against the background of 1965. Way back then, in the old days, Jagger was able to add a touch of defiance and social protest to the overwhelming frustration he and the people he spoke for justifiably felt. But this is 1969 now, nearly another whole generation later, when the hope that came out of Haight Ashbury is nearly dead, when the protest has been neatly swept up and glossified by the mass media ... If 1967 was the year of the Beatles and 'Get Together', if 1968 was the year of The Band and *Beggar's Banquet*, then 1969 may well be the year of The Stooges. You might not like it, but you can't escape it."

Meanwhile, the notoriety of The Stooges, and specifically Iggy Pop, was building quite nicely thanks to articles like to following, this one written by Mike Jahn for the *New York Times*. "You never know what is going to happen at a Stooges concert. They climaxed their performance at a college rock festival with Iggy carrying one of the fans away on his shoulder. She turned out to be the daughter of a horrified dean. Says Elektra Records, for whom they record, 'They are not called The Stooges for nothing.'

The group is more important visually than musically. Musically, they fill up the room with very loud sounds and keep it going while Iggy does his routine, whatever his routine happens to be on that particular night. Musically, the image presented by the phrase "a wall of sound" is appropriate. The Stooges' music, for all practical purposes, is one big noise that throbs. The parts are at first indistinguishable from each other. The important thing about their music is that it fills the room and provides a context for Iggy Pop, who is watched by the audience with intense fascination.

Jahn then finished the article with a paragraph that included the line, "Surprisingly, The Stooges make fairly good records." As irritating as this turn of phrase is, the opinion wasn't uncommon among the mainstream. Most people hated them, and even the most open-minded of critics could only accept them as an exercise in voyeurism. The fact that they occasionally had to admit that the music was, if not great then bearable, was something that they begrudged.

The Stooges' debut album has gone down in history as a bona fide classic, and quite correctly too. But still, it was on the live arena that they excelled and those songs really came into their own. Reporting for *Creem* in 1970, Anne Moore would say that, "The Stooges were a dare. We've heard of you, now let's see how great you are. We've seen the best at the Whisky A Go-Go. We've seen Little Richard swagger on out and Morrison fall off the stage. Dare you Detroit boys to do better … the music had the remembrance of seeming sameness, but then who listens to the flutist when the cobra dances?"

Seeming to imply that Iggy's dancing and writhing was a welcome diversion to the monotonous music, Moore sounds less a Stooges fan and more an Iggy watcher, but again, she wasn't alone. The Stooges were becoming a hit with many people simply because their frontman was so watchable. The legendary writer Lester Bangs was another Iggy-phile.

The writers of 1969/1970 may be able to give some insight into the opinions that the music press held of The Stooges around that time, but it's very difficult to convey just what they meant to people. It's impossible to pass on the reaction that a Cream-loving public had to this bunch of conventionally untalented group of 'punks'. And as I wasn't around at the time myself, it's impossible for me to fully comprehend what a turbulent Detroit, never mind the rest of America and later the world, made of kids who were seemingly just making a racket. For starters, it's nigh on impossible to take a band seriously if they're playing a vacuum cleaner or food blender on stage. Just try it. If any bands out there are brave enough, try walking on stage and setting up your vacuum. Audiences would laugh and critics would dismiss you as a novelty act. This is the battle that The Stooges faced, and a battle that they would ultimately lose until way after they'd split up. Also, as you've already read, Iggy's abilities as a performance artist and mesmerising frontman would work as much against them as for them. Critics would regularly accuse them of using shock tactics as a distraction to the fact that they couldn't play and/or had no songs. This is, of course, nonsense and completely insulting to Iggy's overall concept of a performance that affected all of the senses. As Michael Davis has already said, The Stooges started out on stage, not with a well-honed set list consisting of ten songs or so that had been rehearsed over and over again, but instead with a few ideas, the nucleus of something that might or might not work. They would then start with maybe a riff, a drum beat or a bass line, and see where it took them. But here's the trick: even when they literally had no songs, even when they were sat making improvised noises with appliances in people's living rooms, with little to go on except whatever noises the guy next to them was making, even then, they were a mind-blowing experience … most witnesses of those shows attest to the fact that an under-rehearsed Stooges with no songs or obvious talent were an incredible live band. The question was, what could these guys do with real songs? Were they a novelty, destined to remain an anecdote for a few Detroiters to recall at future parties? 'Remember that fucking band with the vacuum cleaner and the singer who threw himself around? What the fuck happened to them?'

The impact that the debut album would go on to have, not just at the time of release but decades later, was absolutely incalculable. The Stooges represented a risk for Elektra. Maybe not as big a risk financially as the MC5, but a risk all the same. They had just about managed to turn the unpredictable Jim Morrison into a dollar-creating machine. With Iggy, they had a similar problem, but while The Doors had come to the table with 'Light My Fire' very quickly (even if the label did have to insist on it being shortened for the radio-friendly market), The Stooges had their drones and a few riffs. Sure, they had a respectable following in Michigan, but that wasn't going to guarantee national success. In retrospect, however, much the band may deny it, bringing in John Cale was a move of pure genius on behalf of the label. While they had their inevitable clashes, as a group of artists this headstrong were bound to have, Cale knew from his own experience how to pull something listenable and maybe even melodic out of an initial melée of art, rock, dust, dirt and filth. When Cale told the band to turn down their instruments, he wasn't asking them to compromise their art and integrity. Rather, he wanted the record to showcase exactly what this group of four men were capable of. The volume and distortion can be sorted during the mix. And as for the final mix? While some feel that it sounds under-produced and tinny, most Stooges feel that Cale (and Holzman) perfectly captured the feel of the band. Now, any such arguments are irrelevant because it's done and this is what the record sounds like, like it or loathe it. The fact that it divided opinions, and continues to divide opinions, in the way that it did would have pleased the band no end. Lenny Kaye summed this train of thought up beautifully in his *Fusion* magazine review. "I was once thinking of doing a piece on Blue Cheer [the San Francisco-based psychedelic rock band] where I wanted to show, through all sorts of diagrams and convoluted logic, that given the context of their chosen field, i.e. 400-decibel tasteless rock, they were actually Unrecognised Masters of Form.

While I never got around to formally putting the thing on paper, it did start a whole train of thought about Good and Bad, and how generally recognized musical standards could and should be thrown out the window under certain conditions. The key, it turned out, was really in what the group was (consciously or unconsciously) attempting to do, and whether their music mirrored this and made it work …

Like the Velvet Underground or the Seeds [a renowned pre-punk band of the same era], or a select number of other bands, any formal criteria here become basically irrelevant in the face of what is actually happening within the music. All the above factors, negative though they seem, ultimately become necessary to the success of the Stooges, to the emotional set of moods they are trying to portray and, in consequence, they all work within the context the group members have set out for themselves." Always reliable for good copy (and some great guitar licks in his time to – go and listen to *Horses* again), Lenny Kaye was totally in tune with The Stooges and what they were setting out to achieve.

Legendary Detroit shock rocker Alice Cooper would write of The Stooges' debut in the 2007 issue of *Mojo* that, "The first Stooges album was true Detroit music. We played the Grande Ballroom with Ted Nugent, The Amboy Dukes, the MC5 and The Stooges, with The Who headlining. That's not a bad show! But the only band I didn't want to go on after was The Stooges. They would just wear the audience out because they were so good at what they did …

We came from LA and were used to playing with The Doors and Love, and while we were hard rock, we were more like The Yardbirds crossed with *West Side Story* – a little bit more sophisticated. We were listening to early Pink Floyd and Stockhausen. When we put on the first Stooges record, I had never heard an album like that before. I had always listened to bands that were trying to be The Beatles, trying to find the best guitar player or the greatest drummer, whereas this was absolutely anti that.

The guitar player doesn't play anything that he doesn't have to play. There's an amazing lead guitar on it, the drummer is straight down the middle, the bass lays there on that one note, but they're smart enough to let Iggy's lyrics and personality really take over, to be the music and work. 'I Wanna Be Your Dog' is their 'School's Out'. Who would have the audacity to sing something like that? If The Sweet would have done it, no one would have believed them."

As eloquent a writer as Alice Cooper is however, he fails to understand the importance of the Ashetons, particularly Ron, and Dave Alexander when saying that Iggy "totally takes over." Of course, the frontman is almost always the focal point. But, as The Stooges would discover two albums later, they were a totally different band when Ron wasn't playing guitar. The sound that they had (accidentally?) happened upon, that groove that they just lie there on, that had more to do with Ron Asheton than any other member of the band. For many fans, Iggy would never sound as good without Ron at his side.

Scott, too, was crucial. As Alice Cooper says, the drums are straight down the middle. But any drummer will tell you that holding a steady beat over a long period of time is one of the hardest tricks to master. More importantly, for a band so reliant on the rhythm running through their songs, the rhythm section had to have some semblance of fluidity. The 'Dum Dum Boys' shared blood in two cases, and all three had known each other since high school, had played with each other for years. The rhythm section of Dave Alexander and Scott Asheton were very much on the same wave-length, however simple that wave-length may have been, and this fact covers up any technical limitations they may have had. The artistic battle between talent and passion is an age-old one, and it's the people who side with the latter that would certainly favour The Stooges' music. The band wouldn't deny it. Their debut album is the sound of friends getting together after making a local impact, having a renowned producer/musician in the studio with them to steer them in the right direction, and producing a classic as a result. In an era where bands are often manufactured and many artists are little more than puppets for the label, listening to a band that grew and evolved so naturally is still an intense pleasure, even with the benefit of hindsight. We may know what became of the band, but for this short period of time, they were untouchable.

With the album in the can and the reviews mostly favourable, spirits within The Stooges' camp were understandably high. Suddenly the band were getting coverage outside of Michigan, and audiences in other states were getting the chance to see them live for the first time. On the 23rd May, they were booked to play the student union in Delaware, Ohio. The venue that they performed in, the Grey Chapel, had a capacity of approximately 2,500 people but there were little more than a dozen in attendance when The Stooges trooped out on stage. Ben Edmonds [former editor of *Creem* magazine] remembers that "it was a magical performance. The three Stooges just stood there on this huge stage, while you could see Iggy checking out all that space and working out what to do with it. I didn't know any songs apart from one that went 'no fun, my babe', but I was totally mesmerised."

Getting their first album out marked their transformation from local art project to a 'real band'. Now they had songs, magazine reviews and a phenomenal stage show, and the vacuum cleaner was back in the closet. They weren't selling many copies of their record yet, but they were building a reputation as a dangerous band, something to genuinely *fear*. Going to see them play was a real test of courage, and certainly an expedition into the unknown. People got hit, spat at and had gear thrown at them when going to see this band. They weren't for the faint-hearted.

But those that did venture out were treated to a show they'd never forget. And how many bands can really make that claim?

RON COOKE & JOHNNY BEE

There's no way to shape line
with rhyme,
no help from Nymphs or alcohol.
The pressure of glory wears holes
in life.

Viktor Sosnora

During the course of my research for both the MC5 book and this Stooges biography, certain events have transpired that have made me wonder what I'm doing right. Strokes of luck that have added invaluable colour to my work, that just fell into my lap. While out in Detroit on MC5 business, I was able to attend the Grande Ballroom reunion concert at the Royal Oak Theatre. When I booked my trip over there, I had no idea that this concert was going on. Even to a skeptic like me, this did seem like fate. On the bill that day were Third Power, The Crazy World Of Arthur Brown, Canned Heat and Big Brother & The Holding Company (featuring a more than able replacement for Janis). Sadly there was no sign of any members of the MC5 or The Stooges, but I did make a number of contacts that bode me well for my future research. Special mention must go to The Mad Hatter, a Grande legend who, unsurprisingly, wears a big black top hat. I swapped business cards with Mr. Hatter, though it's not until I returned to my friend's house that evening that I noticed that Hatter's card didn't have any details on it — just a swirly pattern. Still, it made me laugh and the fact that I'm writing about it now proves the value of meeting the colourful characters of Detroit like this.

Another person I met that night was a photographer called Richard Peardon. Richard was snapping pictures of the bands as they played and I got talking to him, thinking that there might be a possibility of using some

61

of his pictures in the future. He invited me to join him and his friends at his table for the evening, and we all had a great, slightly drunken night. As well as being a great photographer with a keen eye for a live shot, Richard is an extremely sweet guy. He always seems to be in a hurry, rushing from one place to another, or changing subject matter from one moment to the next. He's extremely likable and was more than willing to help me with my research.

When I returned to Detroit in 2007 to research this book, I spent my first full day at the People's Arts Festival at the Russell Industrial Centre. The Russell is a place that needs to be seen to be believed. Built in 1920, it was originally a car manufacturing plant (like most industrial centres in Detroit), but when its use became redundant it took on another life, incorporating warehousing, office space and artists' studios into its vast structure. Vintage poster artist Mark Arminski has his studio there.

And so, on that first day, I went over there for the Arts Festival. I hadn't planned my trip around the festival; I was just extremely lucky once again. The music ranged in standard from abysmal to excellent, with the likes of Jill Jack and Audra Kubat proving highlights of the day. But the music played second fiddle to the other characters I found dotted around the place. Legendary artists Gary Grimshaw, Carl Lundgren and resident Mark Arminski all had a stall selling their wares, as did photographer (and friend) from the MC5 book, Leni Sinclair. Leni's Kick Out The Jams *movie was being shown on a projector in one of the empty spaces. She also introduced me to MC5 frontman Rob Tyner's widow Becky, and I was able to give her a copy of my book. Becky had been unable to talk to me around the time of the MC5 research, but it was good to finally be able to speak with her. Also in attendance was Richard Peardon, who called me over to a stall he was sharing with a guy named John Badanjek (aka Johnny Bee). I was delighted, to begin with, that somebody had recognised me on my first day in town. Richard introduced me to Bee, a drummer and artist with a huge reputation in the city. Bee had played with Mitch Ryder's Detroit Wheels plus the spin-off Detroit band, which had been managed by John Sinclair. He had also sat behind the kit for The Rockets, Alice*

Cooper (on the Welcome To My Nightmare *album*) and, more recently, local heroes The Howling Diablos. He told me that he had many Stooges anecdotes from their days touring together in the late 1960s. We swapped phone numbers, and I soon contacted him to set up an interview.

Bee is a very intense character, blessed with a dry sense of humour. Before we met up, he sent me the following intriguing email, together with the poem that leads off this chapter: "Now Brett, one day at a ballroom on Jefferson in Detroit. Johnny Winter was the headliner and Edgar Winter was playing with Johnny. J. Geils was on the show, Detroit Featuring Mitch Ryder, Ted Nugent, Iggy and The Stooges, The SRC, The MC5 and many more. And there was only one dressing room for all the bands and their girlfriends or wives. And the story I'm about to tell you, well, we'll have to get together and have lunch. It's a good one though."

How could I not to meet with him after that?

The scheduled meeting took place at his house. Bee always wears a black beret and often wears shades. It gives him an image that merges 'French artist' with 'rock 'n' roll chic', though in all actuality it's just Bee. That's him, take him or leave him. Below are excerpts from the following conversation. It wasn't all easy to figure into my approach to The Stooges' story, but it was certainly too good to leave out. Bee provides an image of that era in Detroit that I wouldn't have been able to.

BC: *Do you remember first hearing The Stooges?*
JB: "You're going back to the late 1960s. They were local bands. We weren't local by then, we — Mitch Ryder and the Detroit Wheels — were one of the first bands to have hit records. We were on *American Bandstand* in '64, '65, '66, etc. These bands came later, The Stooges with the MC5, SRC [Scot Richardson Case] etc. After the Detroit Wheels, I had a band here that eventually became the Detroit band that John Sinclair was managing. Him and Pete Andrews at the Hill House in Ann Arbor. That's how the association started happening. John was managing the MC5 and we started playing these shows at the People's Ballroom in Ann Arbor with Iggy, Ron and Scott. We just talked small talk. There was a ballroom, I

63

think called the Cinderella Ballroom, on Jefferson. A bad neighbourhood – they started having these gigs there. It was some old ballroom, I'm not exactly sure of the name. Upstairs was all wood. At this one show, Edgar and Johnny Winter were headlining. I think SRC and Frost were on the bill. Maybe J Geils too. There was only one dressing room for all the bands. We play our set – Detroit featuring Mitch Ryder. I walk into this dressing room and I'm soaking with sweat. The room is square, 15ft x 15ft. I'm trying to get in a corner and get changed. I hear 'Ooh ow', and I look and there's Jim. He's got his blue jeans on, and these girls have a jar of peanut butter and two knives, and they're making him a peanut butter shirt. That was his stage outfit. BUT they got crunchy peanut butter. So they're smearing it into his skin and the nuts are digging in. He's bleeding and yelping. He's got the whole shirt of peanut butter, sleeves and everything. He's going on stage like that. And they went and got crunchy. I always thought that was a great story. I'm going 'What is wrong with you?' He says 'They're digging these peanuts into my skin. The girls are going 'Well, they won't stay on' and they're pressing these knives to his back. To me that's one of the great Jimmy stories. What am I gonna wear on stage tonight? I know, I'll wear a peanut butter shirt. Of course by the third number, the peanut butter has melted onto his pants and the stage.

Later on, in '75 I was doing a Dr John album. Bob Ezrin was producing it, who would go on to produce The Wall. He wanted me to play drums on it and I went on the road with him. We were playing in The Rockets seven nights a week in Detroit. We were taking a break. [Someone] tells me that Ron Asheton is living on the Sunset Strip in an old apartment building where a lot of aging actors and actresses lived, and he said to stop by. I said that we'd go by one afternoon. We go by there one afternoon, paint's peeling off. We get to Ron's place and this young black kid opens the door. He goes, 'Ron just went back to Michigan county. But c'mon in please, c'mon in.' I'm looking around at Ron's apartment and he's got all these uniforms and daggers all over the wall. I'm not feeling good about this place, and I say that I have to get out. The place was just covered. There was a dummy there with an SS uniform on. I have to get

*out of there. I told Ron that years later. He says, 'Oh yeah, I heard about
that. You didn't stay long!' It freaked me out. I'm always freaked out
anyways, but that really freaked me out.*

BC: Can you remember first hearing The Stooges?
*Ron Cooke: "They're well known for being rudimental. Were we behind
the 8 ball? No way. I belong to the players club. It might not be the most
famous fucking thing in the world, but I belong to a select group of cats
who can literally play their axe in any situation. Any kind of music. I'm
an arranger. There's rock stars and then there's the player's club. Those guys
are good at what they do and that's what they do, but they're one thing
and one thing only. But God bless 'em, they're doing well and that's cool.
The famous thing about me and Rock is that it was hard for me to play
with him after playing with a guy like Bee. He's one of the greatest
drummers in the world. But I did, I went and did that, and I socked down
in that pocket out of due respect for Fred. I did the recordings and I did
those live recordings with them.*

*After that I was in The Brothers Of The Road band with Scott
Morgan, and Scott Morgan's brother on drums. With Scott, the other guys
made a big deal out of it but I didn't, the fact that Scott was in any way
shape or form an inferior player. I did what I did and I got done with it.
They said that I traded my guitar for a motorcycle but that's bullshit. That
I was calling up and borrowing amplifiers? No man. You want me to play
there, have an amplifier there. I'm not calling up and mooching an amp.
Fuck you. Don't make me look like I'm some sort of fucking mooch, that
ain't the fucking truth. When I hear the recordings back with me and
Scott, I go fuck yeah. We made each other sound pretty good. I like to
think that it's a credit to my ability to down play and make everybody
sound good around me. It's what everybody will tell ya. That guy can
make shit sound good.*

*Ronnie's a real personable cat. Scott's quiet. I remember Ron backstage
chucking it up and chatting. We played a few gigs with those bands but
not many. When I was in the Detroit band, we were touring everywhere.*

That band was on the road 200 fucking nights a year. We played a big festival that John Sinclair organised. I don't know if The Stooges were there, but lots of bands played. We were getting encore after encore after encore. The organisers told our road crew that they were gonna shut the power off on us. Our road crew guys said, 'I don't think you wanna do that, man. They're about done. They're relishing the home crowd.' They pulled the plug on us and we beat the shit out of them. Busted noses, busted arms. That was for the biggest promoter in Detroit. 35,000 – 40,000 people were rocking like motherfuckers and the next thing they knew, motherfuckers were falling off stage. When I tell you we were the original leather clad tough guys, we were. That was a big festival in Detroit. Bee was like the union steward. Bee wouldn't get involved in that shit. Some of us would, but Bee wouldn't. It reflected in our lifestyle and our music. We didn't go looking for trouble. We just showed up to party. A lot of people who were set aghast by us, by the time we left town they loved us. Loud music, but we never got to the point where we sounded bad."

CHAPTER 3

B y the time the 1970s began, a decade that saw the end of the 'Summer of Love' culture, The Stooges were starting to enjoy a taste of the high life. They were the band that it was cool to be seen with, the men that the groupies wanted to notch up. Things were going well. Other local musicians may have still mocked them for being technically limited, but The Stooges themselves had no reason to give a shit.

While models were hanging off Iggy almost every time he went out, he actually chose the company of 14-year-old Betsy Mickelson. The singer even managed to charm Dr Mickelson, Betsy's father, which can have been no mean feat. Ron Asheton: "She ruled the relationship in a lot of ways, and he enjoyed that."

Girl issues aside, the band were already starting to think about their second album, before the dust had even settled on the first. Dave Alexander was starting to have more input into the writing, notably coming up with the riff to the song that would later become 'Dirt' and the bass line to 'Fun House'. The band as a whole were on something of a creative wave, a stark contradiction to the problems that they'd had when writing songs for the first record.

Speaking to the author, Ron Asheton said: "After we did the first album, it was straight off to promote and on the road. Like, 'You've got a record out, you've got to play.' It wasn't that long. One album has 1969 on it, one has 1970 on it. It was one year. I think we just got under the wire with 1970. We just went out on the road and played and played and played. The songs were written on little breaks and incorporated into the show, until they were songs that were being played.

It was a learning process. We were playing all the time – we actually learned how to play on the stage. It wasn't sitting at home, it wasn't being in the practise room, it was actually on stage. Just by sheer repetition, by shows, play, play, play. You can tell that we had progressed. Everyone's a little bit more knowledgeable and fluent on their instruments. We were able to express ourselves. At least for me. I was able to express myself and get out more of the things I wanted. But I still love the first record for what it is. Not that I dislike it. But you are what you are. You move ahead. There were simple things, like I went from playing a Flying V to playing a Stratocaster. Still using Marshalls. Like anybody who keeps on playing music, you always learn, you always get better every time you play up until the day you die. That's the way most musicians are."

Owing to Iggy's issues with John Cale's production work on the first album, the band were in need of a producer for their sophomore album and Don Gallucci was chosen ahead of Jim Peterman (of The Steve Miller Band) and Jackson Browne. Another welcome addition to The Stooges' family around this time was Detroit saxophonist Steve Mackay. Speaking to the author, Mackay explained more: "I started playing when I was nine in public school. Back then, more schools had bands but not many do now because they can't afford it. I was very fortunate to learn how to play and I stayed with the school band program until, I guess, [I was] 14 or 15. I had this wonderful man teaching me. We also had a marching band which you had to be in if you wanted to be in the stage band. The stage band was the one that did all the big band arrangements and stuff like that. I wanted to play baritone sax and so that was the way to do it. After a year of that, what you'd call our ninth grade, I came back after the summer vacation and the old teacher was gone – he couldn't afford to be a music teacher anymore and send his children to the same school. They got a young guy right out of college and all he knew about was marching bands and concert bands. He said that we weren't going to have a stage band, so I quit the program. That happened to coincide with the British invasion, so all my friends started getting guitars and things like that. I ended playing saxophone in a group like that – it was called Chaos Incorporated. We started out very simply and we did a lot of covers from the day. We had that band for about three years and we ended up playing all over the lower Michigan area. We made pocket money from that. One day I was going into rehearsal during the early days, going down to the basement, and I heard a couple of the guys talking. One of them said, 'We don't want a sax in the band. Nobody has a sax in the band.' Then another voice said, 'Yeah, but he's the only one who can play a lead.' I just pretended I didn't hear and I walked in and said, 'Hi fellas, how are ya? Let's get to work.' So that happened and that was wonderful. Then I went to the University of Michigan. My parents said, 'Would you wait until the second term before you joined a band please?' and it took me five days to join a band. That was called Billy C and the Sunshine. We used to rehearse right over the street from where The Prime Movers lived. Our keyboard player was Bob Scheff, now known as Blue Jean Jeremy. We played in that band for about three or four months and then Billy C left. He went on to join Commander Cody, some other friends of ours. We started another band called The Charging Rhinoceros Of Soul. We did a lot of R&B covers – Otis Redding and stuff like that. I did that for a couple of years while I was going to school. I quit that because I got tired of the structure of it and wanted to do something more experimental, so a friend of mine and I started Carnal Kitchen. This started out as just sax and drums, then we got other people in on it. We would just basically improvise. That band ended up having several different incarnations, but at the very first [night] we played, I looked in the crowd and there was my acquaintance and fellow band leader Iggy Pop. I had seen The Stooges before and thought they were great. He ended up approaching me at the record store where I worked, and where he had also worked actually, and he said, 'Come on out to the house and jam with us.' I went into there, and they had '1970' and 'Fun House' all ready to go. He said, 'Play some kind of a James Bronwick over this song, 'Fun House''. I played a couple of gigs with them, and was then informed by the crew that we were going to LA. That was when we did the *Fun House* album. I thought it was very interesting. There were all kinds of interesting bands but they were the most experimental. I guess Iggy was attracted to wanting to work with me because he could see I had a free jazz thing going on. The certain lack of structure was appealing. Being in something that was happening was appealing because they'd already had one record out by then."

A freeform jazz aficionado like Mackay with The Stooges doesn't instinctively seem like a good fit, especially when considering Mackay's musical expertise when compared to the other band members, but in fact the combination of the musicians worked beautifully. In many ways, Mackay would seem more suited to the jazz-loving MC5, but he wasn't keen. "I learned to like [MC5]. When I started out with Billy C And The Sunshine, we would be at the Grande Ballroom on a bill with them very often. Frankly, it was a little bit too loud for me. Even when I started playing with The Stooges, it took me a little while to come around to the tunes, but once I started hearing the tunes I was really impressed. They had a nice structure to them, even though they were simple. I liked the 5. They rehearsed in my basement one time when they were waiting for their gear to come back from California. We were fairly close, but they never asked me to join their band. I think things worked out for the best."

Mackay does remember his first show as an honorary Stooge. "I think it was at a place called The Octagon in suburban Detroit somewhere. I think that was the first show, although I may be wrong. It was whichever show they had that weekend. They said, 'Now, we've played these songs, come to the gig and sit in with us.' Then when I went to LA, it was, 'Come down and lay some tracks down and it'll be six weeks.' Six weeks turned into a memorable six months! By the time that run was over, I was basically glad to get back to my job at the record store because things were deteriorating. It was a better influence for me to not be around those guys." Mackay simply decided enough was enough and parted company with The Stooges in October 1970.

He treasures the memory of working with Dave Alexander. "Oh, Dave was a sweetheart. When we were doing the album, I had a really good chance to get to know everybody. That was over on the cheap side of the motel. I had a single room, and the crew guys had to double up. The main guys in the band each had a little poolside apartment. We'd get up in the morning and have breakfast at Duke's Coffee Shop downstairs where Jim Morrison would eat his breakfast. I found I missed him by about an hour every day because he was coming in later than me. I would go over and visit Danny Fields or Ron, Scott, Jim or Dave. Hang out for a while. Dave was a wonderful and gentle soul."

Ron, too, was a pleasure to be in the studio with, according to Mackay. "He was fine. That whole session took a certain amount of time. I played a total of maybe four or five sessions, and I would go in and do overdubs, except for 'LA Blues' which was done completely live, and there were a couple of takes of that. Ron was great to work with. He played his parts, Scotty played his parts and we didn't talk about the music that much. We would just go in and do it, and I spent much of my time with Don Gallucci and [*Fun House* producer] Brian Ross-Myring on the other side of the glass. I'd like to say that I made a couple of suggestions that were followed up!"

John Sinclair: "Steve Mackay was a friend of mine, still is. I knew him from the Carnal Kitchen and a few other bands. He was an energetic character, although not as much as he is today, and a very fine player. He knew jazz. He's a great guy, I liked him a lot. I thought bringing him in was a smart thing to do. Although there's only so much you can do with them little drones. I think he was a big part of *Fun House*, although I've got to say that Jim probably had the whole concept in mind before he walked into the studio."

The Stooges' second album, *Fun House*, was released in July 1970. 'Down On The Street' opens the record, and it continues pretty much exactly where the first album left off. It's a song that stirs a thousand images as Iggy sings 'Down on the street where the faces shine', it's impossible not to see the many characters that inhabit the streets of Detroit, or possibly LA where the album was recorded. But it's the line 'I see a pretty thing – ain't no wall', followed by the repetitive use of the phrase 'no wall', that is most indicative of Iggy's personality. He really did have the ultimate confidence in his own abilities to get women. Ron plays a sexy, dusty riff throughout, and really lets rip during the climatic, though short, chorus. The rhythm section do their stuff with a predictable lack of fuss, maintaining a steady beat and bass line throughout.

'Loose' is the second song on the record, and if 'I Wanna Be Your Dog' was the sound of the band discovering how to be raunchy, 'Loose' is the same set of guys gleefully embracing pure filth.

There's no hiding the joy in Iggy's voice when he sings the line "I'll stick it deep inside", and Ron pulls out a suitably sleazy riff to match.

'TV Eye' is next, a song that Kathy Asheton explained was about the look a person gives to somebody they're attracted to. The 'cat' that is the subject of the song is apparently on her back, with a TV Eye on Iggy. It's fair to say that The Stooges weren't always subtle.

'Dirt' brings the tempo right down, but it's no less exciting with Iggy asking another prospective partner if they feel the fire inside him when they touch him. 'Dirt' is the band exploring a much more laid back feel, and the song has the perfect name because it really does feel dirty and dusty, an early example of what would later be known as 'desert rock'.

Just as on the first album, *Fun House* contains a song named after the year it was recorded, in this case '1970'. Much faster than '1969' on the debut, '1970' perfectly portrays the band's feelings towards the new decade. "1970 rollin' in sight, radio burnin' up above," lyrics like this bring forth vivid images of the 1970s as a much faster, energetic decade.

The title track is the band's call to arms. It's a description of what they, particularly Iggy, did with their lives when they weren't performing. If anybody was in any doubt about what went on in the Fun House, they knew now. Ian Dury hadn't yet invented the phrase 'sex, drugs and rock 'n' roll', but as a lifestyle it was in full swing over at The Stooges' place.

'LA Blues' is the last song on the record, with Steve MacKay's sax really shining through. The song weighs in at a healthy four minutes and fifty five seconds, and the majority is a cacophony of noise from the four instrumentalists, with Iggy howling over the top like the primal creature that he so often was on stage. At one point, he actually growls like some sort of big cat. The last song on the second album is perhaps the most indicative of what The Stooges of old were like on stage, back in their 'vacuum cleaner' days.

Reviewing the album for *Rolling Stone* in October 1970, Charlie Burton played with the album's title, opening with "Ah, good evening my good friend. Good evening and welcome to the Stooges' Fun House. We are so glad you could come. Oh, do not be alarmed, dear one, if things should seem a trifle unusual ... or, as the natives say, "oh-mind" ... at first. You'll doubtless get used to it. Perhaps, you may even begin to ... *like* the things you see."

Burton seemed to have a surreal time writing this particular review, and it's hard to ignore the sarcastic undertones to his writing. Still, he raises many valid points, particularly when he later describes them as "exquisitely horrible" and yet "the ultimate psychedelic rock band."

Reviewing the album retrospectively for *Stylus* magazine, Patrick McNally said, "By that point, The Stooges could play and they do so *densely*. They still had a childlike glee in everything that they did, but throughout the course of the album they go from being 'Down on the Street' to lost in the streets. Like the debut album, the band played to the limits of their capability, but they were capable of much more. Thankfully their knowledge of when to rein themselves in, so as to temper when they let themselves go, remained.

By the end of the album, which ends in a blizzard of noise and a twin drum-kit freak out, The Stooges are lost culturally and spiritually in the smoke and riots and confusion of Detroit and America at the dawn of the 1970s, but also in the overwhelming squall and clatter of the sound that they – from nothing, from nowhere – managed to create. It seems stupid to have to say something so obvious, but energy plus intelligence plus electricity equals beauty. To have fun, you first have to acknowledge there's No Fun. Raw fucking power."

It's certainly true that the band had become more adept at playing their instruments, and Steve Mackay had added a whole new dimension to what they were capable of. McNally may have had the benefit of hindsight, knowing as he did when he wrote the piece the impact that The Stooges would go on to have. But still, his assessment of the record is spot on and the equation 'energy plus intelligence plus electricity equals beauty' could sum up The Stooges' career.

In the April 2007 issue of *Mojo* magazine, Jane's Addiction's Perry Farrell wrote of *Fun House*, "It isn't sophisticated but The Stooges made *Fun House* just as rock bands were starting to get into big-haired, corporate rock. It's completely the opposite from that. Every song is bare naked, raw. It's an album that sounds like you're ripping open your heart, opening your chest and exposing your heart. Not because you're in pain, just because you want to live so badly that you want to jump out of your skin. There isn't a freer record in existence today.

The music is gutsy, brash, cerebral – the guitar bashed you in the cranium whereas other bands hit you in the gut or the heart – and the album as a whole really did make you grind your teeth.

Fun House proves to me that there's a secret army out there enjoying themselves without facing pop culture or being accountable to it, and they're having the time of their life. It's also the record that told me that our role as musicians is to go from town to town and loosen the mental screws of people. Turn them into fools. They need that. It is a necessary part of living, to escape. After a hard day's work, there is nothing wrong with being a Stooge."

Anybody who has any experience of dealing with Farrell will know that he's an incredibly charming, articulate and astonishingly intelligent man. In the above paragraphs, he summed up *Fun House* beautifully. The album certainly does make you want to leap out of your natural constraints and really live. The songs absolutely do smack you in the head rather than the heart. Most people agree that *Fun House* is a masterpiece.

Colonel Galaxy, future manager of Dark Carnival – a band that would feature Ron Asheton – told the author: "On a trip up

75

north, Ronnie says to me 'Oh God, *Fun House*, what a terrible mix that album has.' I go, 'You're the only one in the world who thinks that.' Ronnie goes, 'Are you kidding? That's a horrible mix.'"

Speaking in *Please Kill Me*, Iggy Pop said, "In April or May of 1970, we returned to Detroit from doing the album in California, and things were changing. Suddenly unemployment was driving people out of Detroit. The whole atmosphere had changed, and we started sliding into hard drugs."

Kathy Asheton remembers a new face in The Stooges' camp after their return from LA. "One night I walked into the house and a total stranger was sitting there. This guy had literally [got] into the Fun House and was hanging around waiting for The Stooges! I thought the guy was a groupie. He knew about the band, he obviously knew where they lived, and he had clearly made up his mind that he was going to be involved with them."

Of course, James Williamson was familiar to The Stooges and indeed the Detroit rock 'n' roll scene due to his involvement with The Chosen Few. In 1970, having spent some time at a reform school in New York, Williamson returned to Michigan and settled in Ann Arbor. Keen to renew old acquaintances, he began sitting in on Stooges rehearsals.

Ron Asheton: "It's true that I got James in the band. We were kicking around the idea of seeing what it'd be like with another guitar player. I was kinda into it. I wasn't worried about anybody stepping on me or anything. It was just something to see how it'd work out. We tried a couple of guys. Bill Cheatham was in the band first on guitar. He actually came back to us – he was the roadie. He was my friend from high school. I've known him since I moved to Ann Arbor, Michigan. It was like, 'Gee, you play guitar.' He would practise [and] my brother Scotty would mess around in the practise room with Bill playing guitar, and he would go, 'Hey, you play. You have a good little style that would fit in with us.' He did a few shows, but he was very uncomfortable. He actually came back to us and said, 'Gee, I hope you guys don't mind but I wanna be a roadie again.' He liked the job, it wasn't stressful, and he just enjoyed driving the truck on the road and doing that thing. [So] we started auditioning other people. We saw several people and most of them totally didn't fit in. We're kind of a hard foot to fit, to find a shoe for. Not that anybody was really bad. Maybe if they were bad, they might have had a better chance because they could be moulded. Everyone knew a lot of songs, but more than anything else it's the personality. Could I hang around with this guy? Could I live in this house with this guy? Is this guy gonna commit to us as much as we're committed to what we're doing ourselves. I heard that James Williamson was in town, and I can't remember if he called up or how we tracked him down, but he came over to the house ... I never knew him that well ... I didn't get to know him that well then. He was gonna be leaving the States. So I didn't really know him. When we were doing the first Stooges album, he was going to a school in New York and he showed up at the Chelsea Hotel. It was like, 'What?' He tracked us down! I said, 'Well, come on down,' and he came by the house. I can't remember what we played, but he apparently impressed us enough that he got the job. [But] we were hitting on bad times. Things were getting a little rocky around that time. I think we probably played no more than a few months after that, and that was pretty much the end."

James Williamson: "I had gone to school in upstate New York for a while but I was back in Michigan. When they recorded in 1969, I was in New York at the same time as them and so I got together with them briefly. I think Jim came over to my hotel room and then we went over to Danny Field's house so I could hear the album. When I got together with the band guys it was a little later, after *Fun House*. I had gotten tired of living in Detroit so I moved to Ann Arbor. Eventually, a couple of us ended up sharing a house together – Scott Asheton, Bill Cheatham, myself and Zeke Zettner."

Speaking on I-94 Bar, James Williamson also said: "I ended up moving up into Ann Arbor, and eventually I ended up moving in with a coupla guys that were in the band, and we ended up hanging out more and more together and starting playing with each other, playing some jams and so forth, and then eventually, that incarnation of The Stooges started falling apart. Bill Cheatham and those guys were never really musicians, they were just kinda buddies of the band, and they just kinda played with the band for a little while ... I sort of fell in with them because I could play guitar, and they needed somebody. We started playing, and that was kinda the last couple of phases of that first wave of Stooges stuff. [I joined] somewhere in the neighbourhood of late '71, '72. So I was only with that wave of the band for maybe a year. After I started, we had Zeke [Zettner on bass] for a while, then Zeke fell out, and we had Jimmy Recca for awhile, and then Jim was all screwed up. Not only that, but I got sick with hepatitis, and so the whole thing just kinda fell apart."

At that point, both Williamson and Ron Asheton were playing guitar. "We were trying to pull it together, but I think it was pretty disorganized at that point. I would not call it exactly a professional rock 'n' roll band, let's put it that way."

Williamson maintains that his inclusion on second guitar was by no means a disaster. "It did work. That was the final line up of that particular Stooges. It worked fine – the problem was that Jim was going through one of his cycles and he just couldn't keep it together so the band fell apart."

With Iggy, Scott Asheton and James Williamson buddying up over their use of heroin, Ron was left somewhat in the cold. Ron Asheton: "I never was into it. It was bad to see everything fall apart. It's just what happens. C'est la vie. My brother and those guys all buddied up. I think everybody, not just those two but everybody including road guys got into it. It was very hard because, what you don't realise is, we'd always done everything together. We'd tried stuff, and I was never that much into drugs. All of a sudden, I'm an outcast. When you don't go along with the programme, especially something that heavy, it's very cliquish. Junkies like to be among their own kind, like anybody. I was shut out, but I was lucky because at that time I had a girlfriend that I lived with and she really helped me out. I had somebody to cling to, and I would be the night watchman for the house to make sure it wasn't burned down. There were a few fires from lit cigarettes falling onto mattresses and couches. So I'd stay up all night patrolling, so when the guys passed out they wouldn't burn themselves. It was weird, especially seeing things disappear like household items and musical equipment. There was no money. I didn't think about it at the time, but I can only imagine how hard it must have been for those guys to be junkies, and to go out on the road and play. I mean, I can only appreciate it now, as I'm older and wiser. But back then, I didn't and it's amazing. I've gotta give them that. You can imagine how hard it is to be that far away from home. Most junkies stay close to their home turf and their connections. Here's these guys out on the road, and they've gotta have their juice or they're gonna be feeling bad. I've gotta at least give them that. They went as far as they could with it, until the point where it was realised by themselves that the whole thing had to stop. They had to get themselves straight and get their minds right. They just couldn't go on. They couldn't function anymore."

RUSS GIBB & THE GRANDE BALLROOM

The Grande Ballroom is an integral part of any story about any band from Detroit during the late 1960s and early 1970s, and though it's widely associated with the MC5 (see Sonically Speaking), The Stooges played at the venue on plenty of occasions as well.

Just as with my MC5 research trip, I met with Russ Gibb, former manager of the venue, over breakfast at a place called Dimitri's in his hometown of Dearborn while researching this book. Dimitri's is a fairly unspectacular diner, mostly inhabited by the elderly, but Russ likes it a lot and the serving staff know him well – they don't even have to ask him for his order anymore.

I like Russ a lot. On the surface, he's a grouchy old man who complains about the fact that his bacon is too chewy (something that he did on both occasions that I ate with him). But he's full of stories about the Grande days and he loves to tell them. As a result, the early part of this book is littered with quotes from Gibb. (If you're ever in Dearborn, dear reader, I can recommend the Dimitri's omelette).

I also took the opportunity during this trip to go and actually see the derelict building that was once the Grande Ballroom. Despite the tragic state of the place, it's still an awesome thing to see. It was somehow reassuring to see MC5 graffiti on the building, though the imposing painted banner proclaiming the place to be the 'future home of Chapel Hill Ministries' was far less welcoming. The Grande has apparently been passed from church to church, with no one actually [fully able] to [complete] the renovations. I peeled back a wooden board in order to put my camera inside and take some pictures, and it's fairly obvious that no one outside of a few junkies has been inside the building with good intentions for a long, long time. It is, quite frankly a disgrace.

Nobody seems to know anything about Chapel Hill Ministries and they don't have an obvious website that shows up on any search engine, but the rumours around Detroit are that the Grande Ballroom will soon be demolished. The fact that the stage inside is still relatively intact and in need of saving will hopefully resonate with some of the people that matter. Even an organisation called The Friends of the Grande Ballroom have, perhaps wisely, become more concerned with preserving the Grande's history rather than its four walls (the roof having already collapsed). Their mission statement is: "To preserve the history of the Grande Ballroom and its physical edifice while promoting the enjoyment of the Art, Music and Culture fostered by its patrons, performers and promoters." Events like the Grande Ballroom 40th Anniversary Reunion Concert, held at the Royal Oak Theatre in October 2006 are a far better way to remind people of the Grande's heritage than redundant campaigns to get a desperately wasted building restored. They continue to do good work.

CHAPTER 4

With Williamson on board, The Stooges began thinking about their third album. James Williamson: "There was a period of time there where the band disintegrated. I was sick with hepatitis, and so I went back to Detroit and just sort of did nothing for six months, and meanwhile, Iggy was tooling around, trying to figure out what he was going to do with himself for the rest of his life. I hear all kinds of things. I wasn't even involved in that. I was sick, so I was out of commission. Maybe about six months into that, he started coming around every so often to visit me and he started trying this and trying that, and eventually he went to New York, he ran into [David] Bowie and hooked up with [Bowie manager Tony] DeFries. I remember one time I had to get out to Metro Airport and meet some guy who was working for DeFries to talk about what we were going to do, and the next thing you know, he's got us landing a deal with Columbia and we're off to England."

Iggy and Bowie had become close after Bowie had become fascinated by Iggy's stage act. The whole story is told, if in a slightly Hollywood fashion, in the movie *Velvet Goldmine*. In Christopher Sandford's biography of David Bowie, *Loving The Alien*, he said of the event, "Bowie [arranged] for Iggy Pop to fly to London, where, after a meeting recalled by one executive as 'like trying to dislodge a pit bull from one's windpipe', Defries persuaded CBS to pay Iggy a $25,000 advance for an album. That record, co-produced by Bowie, was *Raw Power*."

It's telling that Sandford, a writer telling Bowie's story and skirting over the details of the debacle that is The Stooges' third album, would refer to the project as an Iggy Pop record, rather than a Stooges album. This is because, to all intents and purposes, *Raw Power is* an Iggy Pop album. The fact that it would be credited to 'Iggy & The Stooges' rather than simply The Stooges is the surest sign of all that the singer was becoming bigger than the band.

When Iggy and James Williamson went to England, they did so without the Asheton brothers, but plans soon changed. Williamson: "We got over there and they put us up in a hotel called the Kensington Gardens, which was a very nice hotel. I've been over there fairly recently, where they've remodelled it, and it's absolutely gorgeous now, but it was really nice then, too, especially for guys like us. So we're sittin' around, trying to figure out what we're doing, and we're being introduced into all these English rock circles that David Bowie's in, and basically, we don't like any of these guys, because we're DETROIT guys, and it's just not our scene. The kind of music they play and the way they are is just not what we're into. So we look at each other one day and I think I was the one who brought it up, I just said, "Hey, we know a coupla guys that know how to PLAY." Ron, in my opinion – I know I've taken a lot of heat on this, and there's a lot of different opinions about this – but in my opinion, Ron was always one of the *greatest* bass players there was, and so I said, "Hey, we'll get Ron over here and put him on bass, and get Scott over here, he knows how to play drums, and just *do it*." So Jim agreed with that, and that's what we did."

Ron Asheton: "I was just looking for something. I always hoped. We'd all been through so much together – Iggy, Scotty and myself – that I always hoped something would happen. I was just kinda thinking about what we [were] gonna do. I would probably play with my brother. But in the meantime, everyone was just catching their breath. I was surprised and happy when I got that phone call. Iggy told me that they'd auditioned like 150 bass players and drummers, and they couldn't find anybody that they felt fitted or that they could deal [with]. He asked if my brother and I would be interested in coming over and me playing bass. I said, 'Sure'. It happened fast and it was cool. I didn't have any money, but I'd inherited by default the little PA system that [was] left behind at The Stooges house when the band broke up [there was no official Stooges break-up as such, they just stopped playing, no big arguments, no big fall-out, they just ceased to be]. I sold those to a company I knew. I only had a serious $200. Here we are off to England. I had to give my brother half of it. You can't get in the country without some money or some voucher or whatever. But I was very happy to do it. I love England, and to be able to spend time there – I was there for like ten months. That was great times for me. We worked our butts off just rehearsing all the time."

Williamson doesn't think that Ron was as bothered about being put on bass as he later let on. "Eventually, he didn't react very well. To this day, I think he has negative things to say about that, but I think at the time, he was happy to get the job, and so he didn't even hesitate."

I remember one of the guys we auditioned beforehand was from The Pink Fairies, I think. There were some of Bowie's friends and different English guys from the era. But it's more than just the way that they played, which wasn't really the way we played anyway.

But to be in a band with somebody, if you're gonna play music with them you have to like them. They were just culturally completely different from us, and they didn't feel like guys we wanted to play with. So in the end, Jim and I were staying at the Royal Gardens I think it's called, and we were sitting around and I said to him, 'Why don't we just bring them [the Ashetons] over here? We'll move Ron to bass and get on with it.' So that's what we did."

Speaking in *Gimme Danger*, Ron Asheton said: "Next thing I know, we're in England in Bowieland, Mainman Boulevard. It went from Bumfuck, figuring out what I'm going to be doing, to going into deeper and heavier shit with political intrigue. We were treated good but different. Mainman wasn't about a band, it was about Iggy. He signed with them… he took it upon himself that he was the creator. We were the ugly side cast-offs of the monster he created."

Of being forced to switch to bass, Ron says that "I felt it was a blow, since I considered myself a guitarist. Iggy was saying things like, 'Eventually, you'll switch over to guitar, we'll get another bass player.' I wasn't thrilled but I wanted to go to England to do something. Just something."

Referring to Williamson as his secret weapon, it was very obvious to the Ashetons that they were now playing second fiddle to the new guy. Exactly what Bowie's role in the production of *Raw Power* was remains uncertain, but all of the reports suggest that Iggy, Williamson and Bowie were all wrestling with each other's positions and this created conflict in the studio. However, this did not necessarily do the album any harm. *Raw Power* is a very different record to the first two Stooges albums, but for many fans it remains their favourite. With Williamson onboard – for many, a far more technically accomplished guitarist than Ron Asheton – The Stooges ditched their dirge-rock sound and concentrated on writing real songs with solos and the like. Speaking of the album in *Mojo*, Bobby Gillespie of British rockers Primal Scream said, "The first two Stooges records are incredible but they're all about groove, there's one chord all the way through on some of the songs. On *Raw Power*, James Williamson comes into the band, and The Stooges start writing what seem to be classic rock songs, great songs like The Doors or The Stones.

Listen to what Iggy did before and after *Raw Power*, you realise that James Williamson is a great writing partner for him. The style of the guitar playing changes with James in the band and Ron [Asheton] playing bass. They recorded in London but I've never thought of *Raw Power* as a London record. It's just a classic American rock 'n' roll record with Alice Cooper-type power riffs. To me it owes more to 'Jumpin' Jack Flash'. To me as an album it represents violence, danger and sexual rock 'n' roll. Even more so than the first two. It's a full-on violent assault."

When speaking of the way the whole *Raw Power* experience was handled, Iggy told the author that, "It could have been worse (laughs). Look, the reality of our group at that time is that we were so out in left-field compared to this so-called, weird mainstream American supposedly enlightened rock industry which was gonna culminate in the Starbucks music culture. Look at the alternatives. A band like the MC5, who were a massive influence on us – they were being managed by a guy who was in jail. Then you had The Velvet Underground, and they're being managed by an artist who makes 24 hour films of the Empire State Building. They've got a chanteuse and they don't want one.

Look at where those guys are today, and then look at the artists handled my Mainman – David Bowie, myself and The Stooges, and John Mellencamp, and the involvement looks better. These people thought of us as art. We would have gotten crushed in the American industry. We weren't meant for that. Everything else that happened that wasn't favourable between ourselves and the people we were involved with in England I think could have been avoided by a little less idealism and more discipline on our part, and maybe a little less frayed. But they were who they were and we were who we were, and that was gonna happen. In the meantime, as time has gone on, look at the artefacts. The fact is, did [Mainman] get us well photographed? Yes. Would we have been as well photographed in Michigan? No. Did they get us, in a sense, well represented on record? Yeah … Was I a complete … I mean, yeah, this would be your classic fucked up kid."

He stops short of calling the experience of working with a new guitarist in James Williamson 'refreshing' though. "Refreshing is not a word I'd use for James (laughs). Noooooo. What was interesting about it was, when I first heard James play, he could really, really play and there was a great energy there – you could sense that. A tremendous authority on his instrument. He did not yet know how to organise his thoughts or how to write … finally, shortly before I went to New York to try to get help for a new addition to the group, he came up with [a] riff, and that was the riff that became 'Penetration'. When he came up with that, I thought 'There's a direction, there's my evidence, and there's a way to go in the future.' It took quite a while before he was able to take the next step and come up with stuff like 'Raw Power', 'Search & Destroy' and 'Need Somebody'. It took him a while and I wasn't sure he was gonna do it. In the interim, we were doing stuff that I had written more, that he just played and [he] made it sound great, like 'I Got A Right' or 'I'm Sick Of You'. But when he did it, I was very determined … I found it a real challenge to match it. To match the quality and aggressiveness of the music, lyrically and vocally. It was hard, and I was very, very confident of the quality of the work when I did it. I realised, 'Oh shit, this is really, really good.' I felt, as the tracks started going down and I heard it back, I felt this sort of relief of immortality. I felt like, 'Ahh, OK, I've made a reasonably immortal recording here.' I knew that. I wasn't the sort of artist that thought that Ginger and Johnny were gonna go out all over the world and spend millions of their lunch moneys on it either."

Lenny Kaye, champion of the band, former *Rolling Stone* writer and Patti Smith guitarist, was typically complimentary in *Rolling Stone*. "They haven't appeared on record since *Fun House* two-plus years ago. For a while, it didn't look as if they were ever going to get close again. The band shuffled personnel like a deck of cards, their record company exhibited a classic loss of faith, drugs and depression took inevitable tolls. At their last performance in New York, the nightly highlight centered around Iggy choking and throwing up onstage."

Well, we all have our little lapses, don't we? With *Raw Power*, the Stooges return with a vengeance, exhibiting all the ferocity that characterised them at their livid best, offering a taste of the TV eye to anyone with nerve enough to put their money where their lower jaw flaps. There are no compromises, no attempts to soothe or play games in the hopes of expanding into a fabled wider audience. *Raw Power* is the pot of quicksand at the end of the rainbow, and if that doesn't sound attractive, then you've been living on borrowed time for far too long."

Opinions on *Raw Power* are polarized and, to this day, many fans protest that it's not a Stooges album at all, but rather an Iggy Pop solo record. The fact that the latterday reformed Stooges don't play any songs from this album attests to this. One thing that isn't in doubt is that the album contains eight of the strongest songs that a Stooges band ever laid down. Concentrating more on classic hard rock anthems than the groove-ridden, feel-based songs of the previous two albums, the title track is a burst of energy that features some amazing fretwork from Williamson. Ron proves himself to be a more than adequate bass player, Scott Asheton hits the drums as hard as he always did and Iggy gives the vocal performance of his life. 'Search And Destroy' is perhaps the most accessible, almost radio-friendly that the band ever put out, while

'Gimme Danger' and 'Your Pretty Face Is Going To Hell' hark back to the classic Stooges sound. The closing 'Death Trip' is a psychedelic freak out of a song that exceeds six minutes but manages to stay on the right side of tedious. Opinions are also divided as to whether Bowie's original production or Iggy's remastered version – released two decades later – is superior. Iggy's version is certainly louder and more in keeping with The Stooges, but Bowie's mix allows Williamson's guitar and, indeed, the songs, to shine, so the matter is entirely subjective.

While in London, The Stooges played their one UK show (before the eventual 2003 reunion), at the Kings Cross Cinema. Ron Asheton: "We went by it recently. We get to go to England so much now, I love it. And one of our last trips, we went by it. It was our one and only illegal show. No work papers. We'd been practising so much, it was fun just to get out and play. That opportunity just to test ourselves before going in the studio. I remember it being a rowdy show. I remember one guy getting thrown out. I don't know what he was doing, but the bouncers kinda brutalised him. I remember the little side door being opened and they threw him out by his legs and arms, flying through the air Superman style. That's pretty much all that I remember, other than fighting over who would wear the leather pants. Iggy had a pair of leather pants."

James Williamson: "I remember that we were excited that we'd get a chance to play because we hadn't up until that point. We didn't know what to make of the London audiences, but we just went on and did what we do. I was a little surprised by the reaction, because it was more of a reaction that we normally get in the States at that time because people were used to seeing us. It was OK. Obviously, there [were] a lot of influences that were created that night."

Ben Edmonds had been a big fan of the MC5 and it was he who booked The Stooges for the infamous Ohio student union show when the band played in front of a dozen people. He would later work for Detroit's *Creem* magazine, and he would help plan a rather bizarre stunt in 1973 when Elton John invaded the stage during a Stooges show dressed as a gorilla. By the time Iggy and James Williamson were demoing material for *Raw Power*, Edmonds had finished at *Creem* and was doing PR work. He offered the duo some financial help in getting the record finished.

Of *Raw Power*, Edmonds says, "[That] certainly had punkish themes, but for the root of that movement you have to go back to the original band, who were the ultimate example of the D.I.Y. ethic that made punk possible. *Raw Power* had more flash and nihilism, which punk also found useful. I can't agree with the assessment of my esteemed colleague Clinton Heylin that the Williamson line-up marked the Stooges' transition into a "traditional" rock band. If that did happen, it happened during the recording of the first album, when the Psychedelic Stooges became the Stooges. Sorry, but *Raw Power* is simply not the sort of album a traditional band makes, nuh uh, no way. James may have been a marginally more skilled guitarist than Ron, but the essential quality of Stoogeness – a fucked-up head full of fevered ideas that the fingers can't quite wrap themselves around – was still front and centre."

Steve Mackay: "I didn't actually [like *Raw Power*]. I liked the songs, but I thought it sounded like it was recorded over a tin can telephone. I had a couple of friends in Ann Arbor, these girls from Detroit. They had an old, cheap Japanese electric guitar. We loaned it to Iggy, who at that time was living in a trailer with his folks. He wrote some of 'Search And Destroy' on that guitar, and then returned it to us. The girls were happy because they then had a guitar that Iggy played."

Reviewing the album for *Phonograph Record* in 1973, Ben Edmonds said that, "This new album by the Stooges – aptly titled *Raw Power* – had the very same effect on me the first time I heard it. It's like your first hard-on or the first time you got really high: an experience so overpowering that it forces new definitions for even the most familiar things. At a time when all our heroes seemed destined to disappoint us, Iggy and the boys have returned from the dead with a feet-first assault that will leave its footprints in the centre of your skull. There's no doubt in my mind that this is the album of the year, and it's only March."

Around the same time, the legendary Lester Bangs was slightly left of centre when writing in *Stereo Review*. "For better or worse, though, time has vindicated The Stooges, and 1973 will see them making a comeback of major proportions. They are possessed of a monomaniacal fury so genuine that it makes the posturings of Bowie and the cheery, beery Alice Cooper seem like something from a Ross Hunter production. *Raw Power* may be too much for many listeners to take. The by-now banal words "heavy metal" were invented for this group, because that's all they've got, and they're brutal with it: rampaging guitar lines hurtling out or colliding like opiated dervishes, steady, mindless, four-four android drumming, Iggy outdoing even his own previous excesses with a ragged tapestry of yowls, growls, raspy rants, epithets, and imprecations. The song titles tell the story: 'Search and Destroy', 'Death Trip'. The ferocious assertiveness of the lyrics is at once slightly absurd and indicative of a confused violently defensive stance that's been a rock tradition from the beginning … whether you laugh at them or accept their chaotic rumble on its own terms, they're fascinating and authentic, the apotheosis of every parental nightmare."

Years later, Iggy would remix *Raw Power*, apparently unhappy with the original Bowie mix. James Williamson isn't a fan of the new version. "I prefer the original mix by far. I have to say that's crappy, but it's better than the one that Iggy did. I mean, he put in all kinds of stuff that shouldn't have been in there. He can do a lot of things, but mixing is not one of them. I don't like either mix particularly. I like the album, despite all of that."

Ron Asheton: "We played a tonne when we came back [from England]. I visited home ... Iggy and James went out before my brother and I. We wanted to hang out here for a bit. We hadn't been on our own turf for about ten months. We picked up the same routine. Rehearsing every day. Then we'd play, play, play. Then we'd do the one show in Detroit. Then we'd continue to play. We played for over a year. 1972-74. It was a good stretch. Then the band broke down because of the same problems again. People wore down. Iggy was mentally and physically exhausted. That's when he told me he had to take a break. So I was trapped in Detroit – AGGHHHHH. We were playing our asses off, but we were only paying ourselves $15 per day. So I didn't have any money. When I came back to visit, I was visiting home so I knew that I'd have a place to sleep and something to eat. I had to raise money to get my butt back out there. By that time, I already had an apartment with a cat. I had to get back home, man. What am I gonna do? I was hoping that the little break wouldn't be as long as it turned out to be – the break between the second death of The Stooges [the first, in Ron's mind, came after the release of *Raw Power*] to when we started up in 2003. I went back and just looked around. James got me an apartment in his building. So I was living in the same building as James, and I would still see James and Iggy. That made me feel like I wasn't totally abandoned on the streets. Even though we weren't playing music together, I'd still see those guys. They went through what they went through."

James Williamson: "A lot happened when we came home. We came back to the States with the tapes, but the mixes that we did were not acceptable to Mainman or to CBS so we were asked to let David Bowie mix the tapes. So part of the first phase was having him mix the album. Then we had to find a place to live, rehearse and so on. Actually, probably for the first six to eight months after we got back from London, we only played one show [contrary to what Ron says of their return to live action in

Detroit]. That was the Detroit Ford Theatre. Once we had done that, we got into all kinds of stuff with falling out with [Mainman's main man] Defries, the band were fragmented a bit, it took a while before they came back around ... that's why we started touring – because we needed the money.

It was a great tour. It was extremely hard, it was extremely fun, and it was one of those things where you're hand to mouth but you're enjoying what you're doing. I think the band was pretty cohesive and everybody was pulling their own weight. After about a year of that, it wears you down. I think by the end of that tour, a lot of things had happened, some of which are captured on *Metallic KO* [the legendary live album released later, on which the listener can actually hear the sound of bottles smashing]. But I think by the time that had all occurred, everybody was ready to pack it in.

That [*Metallic KO*] show was a little scary. The night before was far more scary, when we were at the Rock 'N' Roll Farm. That's when it was scary, because it was a very small venue. Iggy went out in the crowd and did his thing, and this guy just stepped up and cold-cocked him. There were a lot of them, so we weren't sure we were getting out of there. But we did, and the next night we were hyper-alert to all of this. But we're crazed. We taunted these guys on. There were a lot of people throwing stuff at us and so on, but on the other hand we egged them on."

After the indignity that Ron Asheton suffered in being demoted to bass duties, the break up of the band, when it eventually came, was no surprise. After a disastrous concert in front of motorcycle gang the Scorpions, the 'final' Stooges gig took place on home turf, at The Michigan Palace. The band enlisted the help of another motorcycle gang, God's Children, as security (echoing The Rolling Stones' tragic Altamont experience). Nobody died here, but the bikers only added to the air of violence. Projectiles flew through the air, while Iggy antagonised the baying crowd.

Hiawatha Bailey: "All of a sudden this Johnny Walker bottle lands on stage and smashes. That's when James Williamson stomps off. Rock was cracking up, he thought it was hilarious. Ron went 'I agreed to join the band again but not to get killed onstage, Jim. This is bullshit.' Iggy goes, 'See what you've done now? We were gonna play our new material but you've pissed everybody off now so we're gonna do a 20-minute version of 'Louis Louis'.' It was the best version of 'Louis Louis' I ever heard.

I got a phone call from Iggy once. He wanted me to go by Stooge Manor and pick up some stuff. This was after he got back from working with David Bowie. When I got over there, Ron could not believe that the last place he had seen Iggy was some gig that he had done a press conference for. The next thing, Bowie and Rick Derringer had made Iggy an offer that didn't include the whole band, they only wanted him. That's not the way we do things here in Detroit. When people are selecting members of an ensemble and taking them away for fame and fortune, leaving the other members back here, that really did a lot of harm. I think that's where Ron's distance came from."

With the band's music lost on a knuckle dragging crowd, many in attendance were convinced that The Stooges were over. And, for now, they were right.

JERRY VILE

Jerry Vile is a name that kept cropping up as I continued my research. An old friend called Scotty Ross, formerly the road manager for the band Gold Cash Gold and now a writer with Clear magazine, told me that I had to speak to Jerry if I was going to get a complete picture of the punk rock scene in Detroit around the time of The Stooges and immediately afterwards. I spoke with Jerry on the phone and made arrangements to meet with him.

Before that however, he had an art opening at the Bohemian National Home Gallery. Jerry, you see, is a respected artist as well as a writer. The opening, tagged 'The Importance Of Being Vile' was a hoot. Danielle Arsenault, of the band Crud (more of whom will come later), unveiled three new pieces by Vile. There was smelly cheese on sticks to pick at, and a cage of rats adorned with small, rat-size pieces of art. Jerry himself was wearing a beret with a large feather sticking out of it, and he yelled 'BEHOLD' while pointing at his work. This was a guy I needed to speak with.

Vile used to be the singer in punk band The Boners, but he is perhaps more famous for the fact that he edited Orbit magazine. Orbit was well known in Detroit for making fun in as outrageous a way as possible out of anyone and everyone who was a name around town. They'd give restaurants awful reviews, but worded beautifully. They'd run lists of the 'worst dressed people around town'. They were horrible to everyone, and proud of the fact. Quentin Tarentino was and is a big fan of Orbit, and he can be seen wearing an Orbit t-shirt underneath his dressing gown in Pulp Fiction.

My afternoon with Jerry couldn't have gotten off to a worse start. When I arrived at his house, no one was there. I called him and he told me that he was three minutes away. Desperate to pee, I scrambled beneath his fir trees and took a leak within the prickly branches. And that's when Jerry and his good lady Kim arrived home. My reasons for being there were entirely obvious when the two of them saw me emerging from the trees.

The Stooges circa 1970.
Michael Ochs Archive/Getty Images

Scott Asheton with Rob Tyner of MC5, 1969.
Leni Sinclair

Dave Alexander backstage at the Birmingham Palladium, USA, 1969.
Leni Sinclair

The Stooges, 1970.
Chuck Krall/Michael Ochs Archive/Getty Images

Iggy with the Scott Richards Case at a free concert, Michigan, 1971.
Leni Sinclair

Former member James Williamson with Patti Smith & Iggy
backstage at The Whisky, LA, 1974.
Michael Ochs Archive/Getty Images

Rock and Scott Morgan after a SRB gig at The Second Chance, August, 1977.
Sue Rynski

Ron Asheton jamming with musicians who later became DAM.
Bob Crawfod's farm, Ann Arbor, May 19, 1977.
Sue Rynski

A very early DAM practice session with Mike Davis and Ron, 1977.
Sue Rynski

Ron Asheton backstage at the MHK
Auditorium, Cleveland, December 3, 1977.
Sue Rynski

Rock Action and Wayne Kramer catching-up at The Second Chance
in Ann Arbor after Wayne's recent release from prison, 1978.
Sue Rynski

Scott Asheton at The Second Chance, Ann Arbor, 1978.
Robert Matheu/Retna

Scott, Iggy and Ron in Michigan, 1981.
Robert Matheu/Retna

Mike Watt, Scott Asheton and Iggy, still rocking, Reading Festival 2005.
David Atlas/Retna UK

Backstage at the Rock and Roll Hall of Fame induction ceremony, March 2008.
Theo Wargo/WireImage/Getty Images

"You didn't take a dump in there did you?" asked Jerry. To his credit, he gave me a lifeline there. I hadn't taken a dump, and almost anything I had done after that would pale in comparison. "I was chasing a squirrel," I said without a hint of irony in my voice. But they knew. They knew.

After that, the day got a lot better. We went for a drive for lunch, but made a detour into Marvin's Marvellous Mechanical Museum. Essentially an arcade, though that description hardly does the place justice, Marvin collects vintage amusement park games and moving figurines. All of them are piled into one small room, seemingly at random, and the various laughing sailors and swinging Humpty Dumpty's give the place a sinister feel. Jerry scowled towards a child that was playing the Family Guy pinball he had wanted to play himself, and instead the two of us played Simpsons pinball. I have no idea who won. I also put a quarter into Zelda The Mysterious, and her fortune was pretty much on the nose.

After we had finished our interview over the biggest plate of cheese fries ever thrown together, Jerry took me to a rummage sale at a church. Yep, you read that right. It was surreal but unexpectedly brilliant hour we spent looking through table after table of crap and laughing. There was one section that was closed off, with eager shoppers having to queue to get in. These were the particularly special items. Jerry and I joined the queue, and when we got in we realised that we were in the presence of… more crap. "Oh, it's all so soft," said Jerry, stroking a knitted cardigan with sharp sarcasm and sending me into hysterics. He also told one of the elderly organisers that I had travelled from England specifically to attend this church sale. I bought a board game called Beat Detroit (which appears to be a Monopoly style game based on the Detroit motor industry – at the time of writing, I had yet to play), a University of Michigan sweater and two t-shirts, all of which totalled $5. Jerry bought a bag of plastic bugs for $1. But the experience was what counted, and I truly laughed more than I had in a long time. If I didn't know it already, I did now. Jerry Vile is a genius. Here are some highlights from our conversation over lunch. Prepare for some of the craziest shit you've ever read …

BC: *When did you first hear* The Stooges?

JV: *"I would have been in high school. We'd always hear stories of Iggy and how crazy he was. How bikers would always beat him up. I don't think they ever played Florida when I was there. My mom's boyfriend was going to jail so he sold her a house really cheap in Fort Lauterdale so he wouldn't lose it. I lived half the year in Detroit and half the year there. Her job was renting the house during season. So I'd go to school here when it was warm down there and it was cold up here.*

I remember in college, fighting with everybody for playing Raw Power. *I lived in a dorm room, and everybody [in] the mainstream population of the time, they hated it. They hated it when they didn't know who it was, and when they found out that it was Iggy, they hated it even more. There were maybe three people in the whole university that liked Iggy. Iggy was something that you could play and drive people crazy, before punk.*

I started out kind of as a photographer, just doing my own magazine which Niagara was the cover girl for and she drew the back cover. She still had a little of her hippie thing. I met Niagara and Ron [Asheton] because I had this magazine. At first it wasn't a real magazine, we just said that we were doing a magazine. But we could get in just about anywhere. We could go backstage. This is when nobody had a magazine, so they wanted us there. We could get back for Roxy Music, and we just totally devastated their bar and food thing while they were playing, just [by] saying we were from this magazine.

I was really a bad photographer. I was always drunk, and I was really cheap. Like, I'd take two pictures a night because film was so expensive. I didn't have really good jobs. I was basically finding enough [for] people to live off. Dividing $200 with six guys. We eventually put out the magazine as a school project for a friend. He did all the work but I got all the glamour. If we were in the paper, it'd be a picture of me. All I would have to do was ask some really stupid questions, like 'What would you do if you were invisible for a day?' People would go 'Why do you only ask stupid questions? You ask the stupidest questions I've ever heard.' So after a while of asking people stupid questions, we got more confrontational.

People treat journalists differently. You can be really obnoxious. There's a local band called Cyniside and he always tells the story of how we went over to his house, and we're big guys too, and we line up cigars in his living room, [in] this really prissy house where he's living with his wife. He goes, 'You light up those cigars and it's gross, then you take off your shoes and your feet smell so bad.' We didn't plan the feet part. They just were naturally bad. I look at all the old magazines and all the old great bands that came by, and we just wrote about our drunken selves. We wrote nothing hardly about the bands. We met everybody on their first tours, and did nothing with them. We could have had a goldmine, and everything in our house got destroyed. But it was fun. Then I started The Boners when I saw how fucking easy being in a band was. Iggy came to a Boners show once. Our drummer was out of town and we had someone else filling in on drums. He was in the audience at The Boners one night, and I was like, 'Ladies and gentlemen, we've got a very special guest here tonight – Chip Zucombi on drums'. We used to play Raw Power *and other Stooges songs, but really bad wedding versions of them. Like lounge music. Before punk, I really loved swing, lounge and 1950s music. New York Dolls and The Heartbreakers would get you into the really old, cool stuff. Iggy came backstage to our dressing room, and instead of being nice and saying hi, I was like 'You're up here trying to steal our songs, fucker. Well you're not gonna find 'em because I've got 'em under lock and key.' He just goes, 'Your songs are too shitty to steal.' I think that's my only real experience of Iggy."*

BC: *You met Ronnie through Niagara …*
JV: *"Ronnie had probably the best stories out of anybody I've ever heard. I always thought that he should write a biography. As far as I know, he's the one that came up with the Stooges' name. He would go and see Larry Fein on his deathbed, and he went out with his daughter … he would talk about how poor he was next to Iggy, and how shitty it was being poor. He could captivate a room with his stories. He was a sharp dressed guy half the time, and then he'd be in some uniform!"*

CHAPTER 5

At a loose end following the demise of the Raw Power-era Stooges, Ron Asheton moved to LA and formed a band called The New Order with former Stooges bass player Jimmy Recca. Initially, the band had The Amboy Dukes' KJ Knight on drums, but he was then replaced by the MC5's Dennis Thompson.

Ron Asheton: "I was like, 'What am I gonna do? I've gotta do what I've gotta do and that's be in a band because that's what I do. I remembered Jimmy Recca. He was the last bass player in The Stooges. James Williamson was the one who turned us on to Jimmy Recca. He knew Jimmy from somewhere and he brought him into the fold, and so I tracked him down. We kinda kept in touch, and I remembered he'd told me he worked for Walgreens. He was travelling with that corporation, doing inventory at their different stores across the United States. That's an interesting and odd job. So I tracked him down and he quit his job. That was a big deal for somebody, on blind faith, to quit their job and their security. But he was ready. He was tired and wanted to get back in. We hung out a lot together at the bitter end of the first break down. So he came to LA and we started up, and I tracked down KJ Knight, who was the drummer with Ted Nugent and the Amboy Dukes. KJ became the drummer, and that was cool. He's a really good drummer, but by then he was like, 'I'll do it for now. See what's happening.' He had other jobs. His parents were players and musicians too. His father played drums and his stepmother was a singer. He liked to gamble, and he also had a regular job as a debt collector. He was making good money. We'd play and play, and audition singers. We found Jeff Spry. Then KJ was like, 'OK, I don't really wanna do this.'

I thought, 'Who else?' My brother wasn't gonna do it, he wasn't that interested. So I got Dennis Thompson. I called him up, because we've always been friends from the past. When he came out there, things really started picking up. He's a real go-getter. He's a mover and a shaker. He likes to make things happen. He likes to have fun, but he likes to work and he's not afraid to work hard. When he came out, butts really started getting kicked. He picked things up a notch, and he was exactly the partner and the help that I needed. We fitted my side of what I do and my approach to things with what he did. We started auditioning singers, and it was actually super-fun. We put fliers and we put the word out. We had a practise room. We'd give somebody that was a maybe/possible an hour or so. But it was so much fun. You can't believe the people that came in to actually want to do this. It was better than any movie, any TV show, any comic book. Everyone was really nice, and there were guys that were total space cadets. It should have been filmed. I wish more than anything that it had been recorded and filmed. Some people couldn't sing at all. We were much better singers. I mean, Dennis could sing fairly well. He could kick out some rock stuff. He's not the guy that's gonna carry the whole set. But the same with everybody else – Jimmy Recca, and I could do a little bit. Not as much as them. But it was so much fun. After a while, we were going, 'This is getting a little crazy. What's gonna happen?' Then along comes this kid, and as soon as he started singing, it was like 'Wow'. This kid had pipes. He could really sing – Jeff Spry. If you've heard The New Order stuff [the band that Ron Asheton would later form with the MC5's Dennis Thompson], he does one side and Dave Gilbert does the other side.

When we were drinking or smoking marijuana, it seemed like he liked to party. It turned out that sometimes he couldn't make rehearsals and we were strapped on the rehearsal time. We were rehearsing for free or next to nothing, because of [studio owner] Bud Ladersitch. He liked us so we got to use his place. He had a regular place over in the valley.

So he left, and then the search was on again, but this time the search didn't take long because somehow it was KJ Knight who called up, because I'd always kept in touch with him. He goes, 'There's this guy I know in town who used to sing with Ted Nugent for a little bit and I played with him. The guy's a good singer. I'll have him give you a call.' So he did. It was Dave Gilbert. He gave us a call and came over. Seemed like he had all the credentials. He'd already played with a pretty major player in Ted Nugent. Ted was out there playing, he had radio hits. The guy looked right and sang right, so we started out with him. We went along with Dave and did the second side of the New Order record. Same thing, this guy sure liked to party. He liked to get high. Kim Foley had helped us out. Always a good adviser and friend. He had set us up some things, like record companies and a booking agent."

Friend of Ron Asheton, Tom Gardener, of the much-respected fanzine *Backdoor Man*, recalls meeting the Stooge for the first time. "Back in the early 1970s, everyone was forming bands. Bands that were before punk, but that would have been called punk bands. We all loved the MC5, The Stooges, the Dolls, the Velvets, Mott The Hoople, bands of that nature. We formed bands of that nature. At one point, all of our various bands had broken up and we got the great idea to start a fanzine, out of Los Angeles. The fanzine was called *Backdoor Man* and it started around 1975. The first issues were pre-punk so we were writing about whatever there was to write about, which was very often heavy metal and hard rock. But also, we were begging for something to happen. Ben Edmonds from *Mojo* was in LA at the time. Somehow we got to hear that Ron Asheton and Dennis Thompson had started this band called The New Order. We were invited to hang with them, so the first time we met we were invited to go on up and hang with them. A bunch of us went up there and set up an interview for later in the week. Myself and one other guy went up there and spoke with Dennis and Ron. Some of the other guys might have been there as well. But that's how we met and through that, Ron and I have remained friends. Through Ron, I met his brother and all the various Stooges.

Ron was a friendlier guy. As everybody knows, he was the one of them who never succumbed to heroin. So he was obviously in way better shape, happy and friendly, and glad to meet somebody who knew who they were. By this time, Scotty [Asheton] was already gone. He had come into town and we had met him a couple of times, but he was back in Ann Arbor by that time. So the only person I saw with any regularity was Ron and my impressions of him were that he was a really great guy, we had a lot of fun together. It was a funny thing because, I'm 50 years old now but I was 17 then. I was like, *Oh my God, I'm meeting this guy who is the reason I play guitar.* It was very fan-based originally, before we became friends. I was almost awestruck. Like, *Oh my God, I'm hanging with Ron Asheton.* The Stooges made me pick up a guitar in the first place."

For Gardener, hanging out with The New Order was a long-running adventure. "The New Order only played a few gigs, and I was there at just about every one of them. Their timing was awful. If they'd hung around for another six months to a year, the punk/new wave scene in LA just busted wide open and they would have had gigs all over the place. But they broke up and left, because none of us knew this was gonna happen. There were little signs of things like the first Patti Smith single, the first Television single and the first Pere Ubu single. Things were happening but no one had any idea what it was gonna turn into. So they bailed and left before they could have really done something.

I can remember going there one time when they were struggling for gigs and struggling for money. Jimmy Recca was their bass player who had been in [a] version of The Stooges. I remember seeing Dennis and Jimmy sat at the dining table practising signing autographs for when they hit the big time. I was a kid, but I could see that wasn't gonna happen anytime soon.

Ron was always very realistic about the prospects for stardom. The prospects for where this band were going. I mean, they were struggling. There was nowhere to play in LA. They were playing anything they could get. It was a terrible time here to try to get a gig or be in a band. They were essentially a hard rock band. They weren't a punk band. They didn't sound like The Stooges or the 5. They were a more generic hard rock band. At one point, they went back to Ann Arbor and Detroit, and then came back with this new guitarist called Ray Gun. In my humble estimation, he ... turned them into a stock metal sort of band ... I remember sitting with Ron at the Tropicana, a legendary hotel here in LA where all the touring bands stayed. It's long gone. Ron was complaining that Ray played guitar better and faster then he did, and that he knew all the guitar theory. He was really being down on himself. I just said, 'Look Ron, he just plays fast ... you wouldn't say someone's a great writer because they type fast ...' Ron still brings that up on the odd occasion. 'I remember this 17-year-old kid setting me straight.' Because he did get real down on himself.

They had some of the oddest double bills. They opened for a reformed Christopher Milk, which was heaven for me because I was a huge Christopher Milk fan. They opened for Judas Priest once. They played this weird festival out in the valley. They did a gig with Paris. One band after another that you knew were never going anywhere. You could understand why they were getting depressed. One thing after another, they couldn't get a decent gig anywhere, opening for bands that were not going anywhere. They used to play this club called the Improv West, which was basically a comedy club. God only knows how they got that gig. These were guys that, if not famous, they were well known. The Stooges never sold any records, but everyone knew who they were. The 5 never sold any records, but even at that point, they were spoken of in glowing terms. I was a kid having a blast, but you could understand why they were getting dejected. If they'd held on for six months, they could have had all the gigs they could have hoped for. Anyone who had a band could get a gig, and suddenly there were clubs anywhere. To be honest, they were basically a metal band and I don't know how well they would [have] fit into the scene, but it really didn't matter at first. There were gigs, and then people were getting signed. Not so much Ron, but some of the guys were getting more and more bitter and angry, and it wasn't a good thing."

Journalist and former *Backdoor Man* writer, Chris Marlow: "I grew up in the Los Angeles area and discovered The Stooges when I found *Fun House* in a used record store. I saw the cover and thought, *I gotta hear this.* A friend of mine worked at the store so I didn't have to pay for it. I could experiment. Then I saw a little bit as time went on, and they played The Whisky. This was towards the end, during the *Raw Power* tour. 1973, maybe. At the time, I was way underage to get into The Whisky. Way underage.

However, I'm not shy and I had the look that I was able to talk my way through the backstage door. Remember what Hollywood was like around that time. I shudder to think what I looked like and I'm glad my parents never saw me. I was already doing some rock writing by that stage, and everybody at The Whisky knew that I don't drink alcohol. So they weren't too concerned about me sneaking in. I wasn't gonna lose them their liquor license. Anyway, I had to see them. I snuck in and sweet-talked the backstage guy. We're not talking tight security anyway. I stood on the stairs that led to the dance floor. It was one of those life-changing moments. He won't remember it, but I kinda met Ron Asheton that night, very briefly. I was keenly aware that I was underage and I had to get out of there before I got all kinds of people in trouble. But I really met Ron a little bit after that when he moved back to LA to start the whole New Order project. The guys from *Backdoor Man* fanzine, including Tom Gardener, introduced me. That's kind of how I ended up actually meeting Ron in any meaningful sense of the term. I got sucked into the whole circle of the beginning of The New Order. At the same time, I was just getting started as a rock writer myself, as and when I could write stuff. I was working at college radio stations and doing the horrible late night shift at commercial radio stations. I've stayed friends with Ron ever since.

I know Scotty, obviously. I knew everyone in New Order. Destroy All Monsters/Dark Carnival singer, Niagara, I knew. She and Ron came and stayed at the house for a while. I have this fantastic memory of coming home and she was sitting in front of the TV set eating an entire half-gallon of chocolate chip ice cream. I have no idea where it went. But she was a lovely house-guest. I went shopping, or I accompanied her as she was shopping, [sometimes] for lingerie. She went to the racier stores for lingerie! So I took her shopping. I mean really, wouldn't you?

Scott'll kill me for this story but I have to share it because it still bugs me. In Ann Arbor, at Ron's house – it's a typical Michigan family home. It has three bedrooms and a garden – you've been in a million houses in America just like this one. The backyard is a lawn that slopes down. A sizable suburban backyard. The whole thing is surrounded by a big wooden fence. At the far end of the yard, on the other side of the fence, is a cemetery. Scene set. I'm upstairs and I hear gunfire. I go outside, and it was cold but not quite snowing. I look in the backyard, and Scotty's sitting there with a box of 'I Wanna Be Your Dog' 45's on Elektra. He's throwing them up in the air and using them like Skeet shooting. I'm an obsessive collector and I'm going, 'You can't do that.' He's going, 'Nobody wants them anyway. Why not?' I managed to salvage a couple from the massacre and sneak back inside, but I don't know how many were shot. I think 'Don't argue with a drummer with a gun' is a good life lesson! That being said, Scotty's always been lovely to me.

I remember the first time I ever went to where all the guys in The New Order were living, because they all shared a place, the first thing I noticed was over the lift button, somebody had carved into the wall '13th Floor' over the word 'elevator'. I thought, *This isn't like where I live.* They used to have to feed the cat, because Ron's cat crazy. They fed the cat in a moat, because of all the cockroaches. They'd put the food in a dish and float it in water so that the bugs wouldn't get it before the cats did. That's the rock 'n' roll dream. I saw a bunch of New Order gigs, and I thought they were great. I loved their music – still do. I wish they'd had a proper chance to get heard.

We're driving home from a gig and Ron's in stage clothes. Ron asks to stop to get cigarettes. I said that I didn't know where to get cigarettes at that time, but he said that the front desk of a hotel he knew would have them. We pull in there, and he's wearing Ron Asheton stage clothes. Leather jeans, knife on his belt, whatever the heck he was wearing that night. And looking as attractive as people do when they've just come off stage. Like, desperately in need of a shower. Picture the scene if you are the hotel night clerk. A car pulls up, this guy looking like that comes running out of the car, with a knife. I'm watching, sober ... I can see Ron running and I can see the hotel clerk, fiddling around under the counter for the panic button. I could see the whole body language of the transaction. But it was Ron's obliviousness to what we all must have looked like!

We went to go see Steve Martin one night, the comedian. He was still playing a little club. There was some folk singer on the bill. We all walked in there looking like we look. I was wearing a leather overcoat thing. Everybody's wearing black leather pants and jackets. There was actually one of those hushes in the room when we walked in. Like, the darts stopped in mid-air. The room was full of nice folk people, and The New Order walked in, who really weren't a folk band. They used to have a lot of fun doing normal mid-West stuff. They used to like going bowling. Dave Gilbert usually had a date and didn't always hang out."

Tom Gardener stops short at calling The New Order a great band. "I liked them very much. At that point in time, there was really nothing going on. Any opportunity you had to go and see any band, it was worth going to see. They were a good band, but not a great band. They had some good songs, but they had a lot of personnel issues."

"There was a big show at the Starwood," Ron Asheton told me. "They liked us there, and we got to play there every five or six weeks. We had our big showcase show, and we got these two girls to watch out for Dave. They bought him this nice shirt, and he looked the part of a rock star. I remember being in the dressing room before the show, and everyone was a little bit nervous. I know I was. I was standing next to Jimmy Recca, when Dave walks buy and Jimmy goes, 'Hey, I smell angeldust.' Angeldust and PCP is the worst shit in the world. Dave goes, 'I'm fine man, I'm fine.' I go, 'Woah wait a minute. You ain't getting high – you promised. That's why you had those two sleazy girls to hang out with all day and do whatever you wanted to do. Take care of you and watch you so you don't get in any trouble.' So we get onstage and we're starting the first song, and then o-oh. He's already sailed by the intro. He was screwing up right at the beginning. We didn't get to do anything. Then he gets into the first song. I don't remember what it was but it was one of our originals. He's singing all diminished, and it just got worse and worse. After a couple, the Quaaludes hit him. Everything hit him at once, and he got booted off the stage.

Then it was, *What are we gonna do?* How utterly embarrassed can you imagine we were? We had to come up with whatever we could think of. Whoever could sing anything. I think Jimmy Recca sang one of our originals. I think we did 'Twist And Shout', we did a Beatles song. But it was just pathetic. We knew we were screwed. And of course, we lost everything. They were gonna make a record. I think it was Mercury. As I remember it, it was something that Kim Foley had set up. But it was up to the old dressing room, and Dave was passed out under the pinball machine. I was standing here like, we're fucked.

[Dave] had a problem – he liked to get high … we came back home and totally bummed out. Took all of his possessions from the apartment and threw them out in the hallway. When he pounded on the door to come back in, we didn't open the door. Just go away and never come back. That was the end of The New Order.

We stayed on in LA to decide what we were gonna do, but by then the music trend was changing. We were catching the tail end before it went on to disco or some other crap."

Thompson: "Myself personally, [back] around 1973, I had a Corvette 1967 that I bought when the band [MC5] sold out. My dad helped me pay for it, and it was a muscle car. A 427, 390 horse power, convertible hard top race car. I sold that for $4000, and now it's worth $60,000, that car! I sold it for $4000, paid my dad off, took $1000 and went to California because I was speaking to Ron Asheton on the phone. Ron said, 'Come on out, I got a great thing going.' I still wanted to play music, so I headed out to California with my $1000. I go out there, and he is with Jimmy Recca from The Stooges on bass and himself on guitar, and a manager named John, his friend, who was using money from a trust fund to support the band. He took the trust fund set aside for his education and paid the rent, bought the beer and the food! When I refer back to The New Order period, I have some great stories. I went out there and it wasn't what I thought it would be. I thought he had this project with a record label, I thought I was getting out there and plugging in. Something that was established. It turns out it wasn't established; he just had some gigs out there and was putting a band together. I had no place else to go and I liked Ron Asheton. I used to hang out with The Stooges – I got tired of hanging out with the MC5 when they started to get really political, at the house in Ann Arbor. They started getting heavy into this political bullshit and I hated it, so I hung out at the Fun House. They were more fun. You go over there and it wasn't about politics, it was about life. Just jerking off, being young and having fun. I hung out with Ron and got to be friends with him. And Scott and Iggy too. Anyway, he didn't have much shaking but he had a backer. We rehearsed every fucking day. Six hours a day in a rehearsal studio, and The Runaways would rehearse right next door to us … Jimmy Recca's bass playing is phenomenal, we're having a good time, we're rehearsing but we're poor. Really poor. That lasted for about two years – in 1975 I came back home."

Speaking of the ill-fated band, Dennis Thompson continues: "That was the end of The New Order because, at that time, that was bad PR to go out. We could have kept going out, but after all that time put in by the rest of to get to that point, to have it blown – I was disgusted and shattered. I just packed up and flew back to

Detroit. Ron stayed out there a little while longer, then he came back too …

There are a couple of bootlegs out there, and we have a complete CD that Ron Asheton put out called *The New Order*. They're really cool tunes. They're rough. They needed a producer. We never really went in and recorded those things properly. I still [say] they stand out. We had a lot of good material. It'd be cool if somebody put out what's available because there's some interesting material in there. Some of the playing is good. 'Lucky Strike' is a great song. 'Victim Of Circumstance' is an interesting song. We never trademarked the name so it was public domain when the Manchester band used it.

I have so many stories about Dave Gilbert. [He] was getting high and coming home late, at 3 o'clock in the morning, and me and Jimmy Recca would still be up waiting for him. He would come home so fucked up, and he would pass out in the middle of the living room. One time, we took all the furniture in the whole fucking house and piled it on top of him, starting with the couch. When Ron woke up, we took his stuff too and piled it on top of him, just leaving his hand sticking out, then we poured warm water in it. He woke up and had to pee, and screamed 'Goddamm, what the fuck'. He had a six foot tall mountain of stuff on him. We were all just sat around smoking cigarettes, drinking beer and laughing. Another time, he fell asleep in The New Order practise room. He was on the floor, and we put the floor tom over his head. All three of us beat on the floor tom as hard and loud as we could.

God bless him, Dave Gilbert died. Another time, he passed out with his guitar on his chest. So me and Jimmy snuck up on him, dropped two cherry bombs inside the hole in the guitar and got a bucket of water propped up on a stick so when the bombs went off he would move and the water would douse him. So we went and hid and the bombs went off BOOM BOOM, the guitar shattered and exploded (it was more than we expected), then the water dropped and he was sopping wet. He gets up and says, 'GODDAMMIT'. Gets up and pisses on the lamp, fries the lamp. That's the kind of shit we used to do in The New Order. We had a lot of fun."

[Here's a] Ron Asheton story: me and Jimmy Recca were the practical jokers. We bought a bag of catnip. Ron was a late nighter, and he came in at about 8pm, and me and Jimmy told him that we'd scored and started smoking a joint. Ron smoked this thing for about five minutes saying, 'This is good shit', before we told him that it was catnip. One time Arthur Kane from the New York Dolls came round. He was a real hardcore alcoholic. Jimmy Recca and I went into the kitchen and made him a drink of every whiskey bottle, every bit of leftover beer we had, Tabasco sauce, steak sauce, ketchup, mustard, salt, pepper, anything we could find. He drank it down and said it was, 'Fucking great, man.' Another time, Ron was pissing me and Jimmy off in rehearsal so we found an old boot in the alley and put it in the soup, and let Ron and John eat it. We said we weren't hungry that night.

We were on to something and we stuck it out. If we had survived, we would have been in on that. We had some names – The Stooges and the MC5 together! I don't know exactly how long we were together, but it was long enough.

Writing songs with Jimmy and Ron was fun. We developed a pretty good rapport with each other. We swapped a lot of ideas. Everybody was free and open-minded about sharing ideas. It was pretty cool. When I got there and saw where we were at – I was gung ho. I was ready to go to work, write some songs and find some singers. We were still young at 26 ...

I'm sure Ron was suffering [after the *Raw Power* experience]. That was a heart-breaking thing for him. James Williamson was living in the same LA building as Ron. Iggy would come visit him, and stop by to see us once in a blue moon. Yeah, it was difficult for

Ron, just like it was difficult for me to be unable to put my band back together again. If he was really suffering, I don't think he showed it very much. He was pretty stoic."

Tragedy would fall upon The Stooges' camp in 1975 on 11th February when Dave Alexander died of pulmonary oedema, possibly caused by alcohol, but there were also suspicions that it was caused by Alexander's eating disorder. He was 28 years old. A couple of weeks earlier, Ron Asheton had been driven by Alexander to the airport and somewhat mysteriously, the bass player had told Ron that it was unlikely he would see him upon his return in a fortnight. Alexander's prediction would be chillingly accurate.

In 1980, Ron Asheton and Dennis Thompson had a reunion of sorts when they formed The New Race with Deniz Tek, Rob Younger and Warwick Gilbert of Australian garage band Radio Birdman. They would tour for one year, releasing the live album *The First And Last*. In the liner notes for that album, Tek would say: "I was living in Detroit at the end of 1980 when the New Race concept came up. This was in the early post-Birdman, post-Visitors days, I was looking around for something to do. It was actually Angie's idea. Angie had been talking with Rob Younger, and she thought it would be great for us to get a cool touring band together to hit the road in Australia ... the idea being to get some guys in it who we considered to be part of our "roots" so to speak ... We wanted to give the Detroit musicians some live exposure in Australia, to honour their legacy. It would be an important step along our own path of development. It would also give us the chance to go wild and behave irresponsibly and kick some serious ass.

I had known Ron Asheton for a few years, and had done some playing with his band. We were, and still are, close personal friends. He was keen on us getting together in Australia. Scotty Asheton was our original choice for drums, but when he couldn't make it,

Ron recruited Dennis Thompson. 'Machine Gun' was a perfect choice for what we wanted to do. Ron and Dennis crossed the Pacific in a DC10, arriving in a strangely compressed state. Rehearsals began. We decided to focus on material from the members' previous bands, to spend the time crystallizing as a unit rather than trying to write a whole bunch of new songs. We did stuff from Birdman, MC5, Stooges, Destroy All Monsters, The Visitors, etc. The only new song we wrote was [about the space shuttle] 'Columbia'."

Contrary to some of the press at the time, we had a great deal of fun, good times, and cameraderie. There was also adversity and, inevitably, exhaustion. Because of the Oz pronunciation of the word 'race', we took to calling the band 'Fried Rice' instead of New Race. Humour beats bitterness every time.

New Race was the hammering out of yet another link in the chain. It served the purpose, albeit unconsciously, of connecting past to future within the context of our limited artistic traditions and humble aspirations. It was better than sitting around watching TV. It was a rock band. Music was played. You can hear some of it on this disc. I hope you enjoy it."

NIAGARA & COLONEL GALAXY

Niagara was the frontwoman in the band Destroy All Monsters, which also featured Ron Asheton on guitar and the MC5's Michael Davis on bass. Because of Davis's involvement, I wrote about the band in Sonically Speaking, *but this time around I really wanted to meet with Niagara in order to get a different perspective of what went down. Jerry Vile gave me some tips for dealing with Niagara before my first meeting with her (of which there were two). I expected to be intimidated by her, but I was surprised to find that I liked her immediately. Her towering husband Colonel Galaxy is a huge man with a well-kept black beard. I met with the Colonel and Niagara at the Majestic Café and I bought them lunch and some Johnny Walker Black label whisky.*

Colonel Galaxy was the man behind the group Dark Carnival, a band which, over the years, would feature both Ronnie and Scott Asheton as well as Niagara and even Cheetah Chrome of The Dead Boys. He told me that he got the idea for the band from a dream that he'd had. He still remains friends with Ron, who had been intimately involved with Niagara immediately prior.

I liked the Colonel. He was a source of witty anecdotes throughout the process, often stepping in to fill gaps when Niagara had forgotten something. He seems intensely protective of his wife, but then why shouldn't he be? He liked me too; enough to invite me over to their house for a barbeque and to conduct the second part of the interview. This was a great result, especially considering that the basement of their house is practically a museum, containing masses of posters, guitars and other memorabilia from Niagara's past.

The following week I went over to their house and discovered a few things about the two of them. 1) Niagara is an amazing interior designer. 2) The Colonel can barbeque a burger like some sort of meat wizard. 3) It is possible to barbeque carrots and they taste good. 4) They live opposite a health clinic, something that Niagara herself described as "handy".

I conducted the second part of my interview with Niagara in her bedroom, while Colonel got the barbeque ready. It all went well and, after the food, Colonel took me down to the basement. A painting of Velvet Underground anti-diva Nico by Niagara adorned the wall, along with various Destroy All Monsters and Sonic's Rendezvous Band fliers [both bands that would feature members of The Stooges later in the story]. One of Ron Asheton's guitars took pride of place, and miscellaneous items like a Niagara cigarette lighter and a Niagara shot glass were dotted around the place. It truly was like a museum of their illustrious past. As I left, they gave me a Niagara t-shirt, a bunch of Punk *and* Juxtapoz *magazines, a Destroy All Monsters/Dark Carnival CD boxed set and a signed Dark Carnival poster. All of this along with Niagara's book* Beyond The Pale, *which she had given us during our first meeting (a kind of swap – I had given her a copy of* Sonically Speaking*).*

One story from the book, told beautifully by Colonel, stuck in my mind. It tells of a painting by Niagara, titled 'Let's Get Some Easy Money', which had been stolen during an exhibition. Colonel picks up the tale: "Flash forward 15 years later: a hot June day. Amir (Daiza) is celebrating an after party for his first annual 'Motor City Music Conference' at his new lake house. Party talk turns to the release of Niagara's book. 'I've got a Niagara painting', says an elegantly dressed lady. 'Oh yeah,' Niagara intones, 'Which one?' 'LET'S GET SOME EASY MONEY' The room gets still as the Colonel walks over to the lady, 'What did you say?' 'LET'S GET SOME EASY MONEY …', 'NO, Honey, we don't own any Niagara paintings', her husband corrects, from across the room. 'But, Honey, this is Niagara! We're going to be in the book!', the elegant lady pleads. 'HONEY, I don't know of ANY NIAGARA PAINTING', emphasizes the husband. 'So that's how we're playing it?' …the Colonel growled. 'How 'bout we wrestle for it now?' 'I don't think that's a good idea', the husband offered weakly, 'We were just leaving.' Long story short: The painting was returned the next day – elaborately framed."

As is now obvious, Niagara is an artist with a considerable reputation, something she started to take seriously during her time in Dark Carnival. Her work can be seen at the 'Cpop' gallery next door to the Majestic Theatre in downtown Detroit, though many of her paintings can be seen in that excellent book, Beyond The Pale. Still, nothing on canvas or on the printed page can do justice to what a unique couple Niagara and Colonel Galaxy are.

One final thing – I wrote something in Sonically Speaking that Niagara took issue with, so I'd like to clear that up now. Niagara never wore baby doll dresses.

CHAPTER 6

When The New Order came to an end, Ron Asheton's next adventure wasn't a predictable one. Destroy All Monsters was a band that had already existed in an 'art-noise' form under the guidance of Cary Loren, when Asheton was invited onboard. DAM singer Niagara has fond memories of first hearing The Stooges. "I was in eighth or ninth grade. We used to have this great radio station called ABS, and I would write in my diary, 'Listened to ABS, it's always on.' They would play Stooges all the time. That was our band. They were gods here. I got to see them in some weird show. One time, I saw them at a Halloween show and I was with my boyfriend who was a senior. He studied Chinese and was really smart. They started grabbing ropes from the ceiling and started swinging from them. Oh God, I was freaked. I haven't been freaked probably since then. Nothing freaks me out. I couldn't believe it. I thought the guy was gonna die or he was making a fool of himself – I couldn't tell which. It was just totally different from any rock band I'd ever seen before. It was ridiculous and death-defying all at once. It blew my mind. I think I was in tenth grade."

Colonel Galaxy: "We had a theory. The Stooges came from seeing The Doors and then a few weeks later seeing the Velvet Underground."

"Scott Asheton's the real thing," says Niagara. "But I think when Iggy met Scotty, he was like Marlon Brando in the movies. Ronnie is really smart, really polite – his father was in the service and he himself took lessons to fly. He wanted to be a pilot and he's still deep into planes ... he's a very quiet person, but alone Ronnie would always say the most audacious things. He's the polite one. When I knew Scott for years, he wouldn't talk at all. He'd get on the phone with one of his friends and [talk quietly] for hours. His mother, Ann, would shout 'Scotty, what's going on down there?' I thought it was so crazy that they were still living with their mother, and then I moved in."

With regards to the origins of Destroy All Monsters, Niagara recalls, "There was two versions of that band. The first was with Cary Loren, and Mike Kelly who's a big museum artist now ... The music part – I don't know what you'd call it. It was an art collective and we were all doing our separate things. No one remembers this but I have the diaries and I crack up when I read it. I was with Cary, and then Mike Kelly and Jim Shaw lived together in this house with other people, this commune. We were all doing stuff together. We never talked about it and one day they were like, 'Niagara do you sing?' They wanted to start a band, like us. Two days later we were playing, so you can imagine how good we were! We kept those standards to the end ... Two days, from inception of the band idea to playing. That just kills me. We were good. We did 'Iron Man' for an hour.

Jim collected outrageous things. His room was full of hundreds of comic books and they had Destroy All Monsters comic books as well as a movie. He was into the 1950s. I saw that name a million times, and then he said it so he must have been thinking [the same]. It was great. It was like a verb, and I liked that. It stuck. We didn't play real shows or anything, we [initially] played in a basement …"

Colonel: "So Cary said, 'We need some balls. We gotta get Ron Asheton, he's back in town.' I got the story from Ron. Ronnie had no intentions of being in that type of scrappy little outfit. But he went to practise and there was Niagara, ethereal as anything. He was ready to get out, and the only way we could get him down was to give him a six-pack! He said that it was like a gypsy thing. Nothing made any sense. Everybody was playing an instrument that sounded like a different instrument. He goes, 'I'll be out of here in about 15 seconds.' Then Niagara walked in and he was interested. She was suddenly by his side and she was popping all these pills. He goes, 'Why are you doing all that?' and she goes 'Because I'm scared to death of singing.'"

Ron Asheton: "It was already a band. It was like, *Oh boy, here we go again.* This time I'm back here in Michigan and I have no money. I was lucky to have a place to stay. What the hell am I gonna do? So I was just kinda licking my wounds and thinking about things, and this guy starts calling me out of the blue. He sounded kinda … interesting. He was like, 'You wanna jam?' I'm pretty weary of strangers calling me up and asking to jam. It's like, 'C'mon. What the fuck?' The guy kept calling and calling, and finally I said, 'OK, I'll do it if you get me a six-pack of 16oz Colt 45 and a pack of cigarettes.' It was Cary Loren. I met him and he took me to this old house here in Ann Arbor. A great big basement, and they had a lot of equipment. I had brought my little Univox amp and my guitar. I listened to them play and did what I could to play, but I'm going, 'Oh my God. This is the biggest mess I've ever heard. Holy cow. What the fuck!' But at the same time, I thought it was *interesting.* Then I started paying more attention and

I noticed that the two guys who kinda look alike are kinda cool. They look real good and they're playing some neat stuff. Cary was playing guitar, and there were some simple things there that I liked. Then Niagara started doing something, and I was really interested in her. I thought *Wow, she's kind of amazing*. I kept looking at her hair. It was all long and thick at the back and then piled at the top like this great big bird's nest or something. She had things tied in it, like bows. She was just being really shy. Anyone that wears sunglasses at night should be a little interesting to talk to. I didn't see any track marks on her arms so I didn't think she was doing heroin. So I was interested. I talked, and I kept going back. I played more with them, and I think I did a show for an art teacher that Niagara knew.

I knew that Michael Davis got out of jail. I somehow got a hold of him and we found each other. Mike was gonna give anything a try for a minute. It's some place to start, once you're out. He found Rob King. I don't know how he knew him. Rob King is a great drummer, besides being one of the funniest comedians I've ever met. A big part of the band was the fun and the laughter he brought. That was the genesis of taking a college noise band, and turning it into a rock 'n' roll band.

Same deal – we found places to rehearse. We found a manager, who was already a friend of Niagara's. We were like his fun little side project while he was still going to school at the University of Michigan. We worked and played as much as we could. Made a living, and worked ourselves into what you can find now on many bootlegs and sanctioned pieces of vinyl or DVDs. [Colonel Galaxy] put out a box set. He's got a pretty good historical overview from the beginning times until the end. The last recordings that we got to do – I was glad. Nobody was going for it. I actually spent [a lot] of my own money to record, to go and get cassette tapes made, to get this industry resource book and mail out hundreds of tapes to every record company in the whole world, and to get nobody to respond, [barely] even a turn down note. We got a few kind turn down notes from record companies like Lime Green Spider, and no one gave a fuck. It was bad timing, but we stuck it out as long as we could. Just like when we toured England in 1979. That was a changeover time. Punk was going away and ska was coming in – the band Madness was really big. Things were changing. We got to do that last tour, and I'm proud of it – the last great ride. It was a fitting end because it was our last hurrah."

Ron recalls the experience of being in a band with his then-girlfriend as different to anything he'd been through before. "It's way different. You can't fire her, for one thing! In another way, it was all good. We had a good time, and between us, our two pay checks made for a good life. We could survive. Niagara will say that it's some of the best times she ever had. She likes material things, but she can go just as well without. She had fun. She really enjoyed the travel and the performing. She's very gregarious – she likes people. Or at least, she likes people that are likeable. Special people. She even said to me now that it's some of the best times she ever had. So it was a good experience. It really wasn't bad. We still keep in touch. I don't get to see her as much as I'd like to or, of course, used to. We're so busy now doing stuff that it's hard. You get off the road and you've got that week or ten days off, you just wanna sleep and take care of your own personal business."

Mike Davis: "I got out of Lexington Federal Penitentiary. Hiawatha was living with us. I'd got into a situation with a young woman and Hiawatha was the room-mate there. We all lived in this farmhouse on the outskirts of Ann Arbor. Hiawatha's a very sweet person.

Ron came out to the house one evening to do some drinking with us, and he brought with him Cary Loren and Niagara. They proceeded to attempt to persuade me to join the band. I think they had someone who was playing bass temporarily in the band, and Ron had it in his mind that to add me would really round things out and they'd get a formidable thing – it'd really beef up the action. Cary was selling it big time. He was talking about what an awesome concept it was and that if I joined the band we'd really be successful and that we'd make more than just the books. We'd really be successful in the business. So I told them I'd give it a try. We got together for a practise, for just a jam together and I decided what the heck. I wasn't playing with anyone. See, I wasn't particularly keen on being in a band any more after my whole experience with the MC5, I'd kind of made my mind up [in] prison that I was going to try and lead more of a normal life. It wasn't in my plans to be a rock 'n' roller anymore. It's one of those things that, once it gets in your blood, it becomes who you are. [So] I decided that I'd join the band."

Niagara remembers those early days of DAM: "That was a beautiful summer, that was a silver summer. We were doing movies; me and Cary were doing all these art projects. We'd go and film mermaid movies in Florida. I was the new chick in town, wearing this weird vintage gear and on this ethereal trip. Mike Kelly sat next to me on the bus because back then, everyone was wearing blue jean overalls. He sat next to me, and right there with him was this crazy freaky transvestite type girl. Ronnie started introducing me to the MC5 guys like Fred Smith, and Ron's sister Kathy. We would go to these parties, and Cary Loren was … really creative!

Cary's playing didn't fit [in a way] with the rest of the band though. He was a flamenco guitar player. I thought he played great. Eventually they all agreed that he couldn't be in the band. It was a bad day when they told him …

We were just hanging out, practising together. We were getting along really good. Ronnie could tell a story that really entranced me. They'd be hysterical, and he'd woo me with them. They were all about Stooges and the past. He was terribly entertaining. There's nothing I like better than to listen to these great stories. He'd just go on and on, non-stop. We kept getting closer, and he always had tacky girlfriends that were trying to be famous groupie types, trying to ride the wave. At the same time, it wasn't like I disappeared from Cary's life altogether. He was coming and going all the time. That was kind of normal but very weird. I just thought I'd be with Cary forever. I thought I'd be dead before now too."

Colonel: "Ron and Niagara had their own hours that they kept. They'd get up at about 5 or 6 o'clock at night, have something to eat and start having cocktails. Scotty would get back from the bar, and then Ronnie would list the things that Scotty ate when he came back. Like, six hot dogs, four hamburgers, two chicken breasts."

Niagara: "That was like 2am or 3am when Scotty got back and we all got along pretty good. The day time was one thing and the night time was different."

Colonel: "Two plates of macaroni and cheese … and then Scotty's belly was out front and he said that he was thinking of getting a jumpsuit, like Elvis. That's Scotty's humour!"

Niagara: "We had our own apartment for a while, but we didn't have money so we moved back. Then we were all there at once for a while. Nobody wanted to see me there. Scotty liked me at first and then was pissed I was there. I can see that. Ronnie and I had a room that I called the Chicken Box, and I just stayed in there. We got along really well for years. Everything was funny. Ronnie likes everything funny. That's what he likes – to laugh about stuff."

Colonel: "Niagara would be telling a story about the night before, about some girl that anybody could fuck. Ronnie would say, 'What did you say? Anybody could fuck her?' And he'd pick up his guitar and he'd make a rudimentary song out of it."

Niagara: "But then any song I wrote, he'd say 'we can't talk about drinking, we can't talk about hangovers, we can't talk about pills!' I'd say, 'C'mon Ronnie, loosen up.' Ronnie may be in The Stooges but he thinks so straight. I mean, that's how he is. His background is English. They're a beautiful family. They've got very straight noses, and when you speak to Scotty he blows your mind because his eyes are like wolf eyes. Very pale blue."

Colonel: At the time that Niagara was putting together Destroy All Monsters, I got Ron out of hiatus, and they started working with him. When Mike [Davis] moved in with me, he started playing bass with them. So my rehearsal space at the farmhouse on Plymouth Road became their rehearsal space. Whenever a touring band was in town like Hugh Cornwell and The Stranglers or Dee Dee and the Ramones, all these people would be really into meeting members of the MC5 and The Stooges. They'd come back to the Fun House and party with us. I remember this one time – one thing you don't do with Rock is knock his hat off. I was there with Hugh Cornwell and this [other] guy … knocked Rock's hat off. Wrong move. Next thing I knew, this battle ensued! Ron and Rock both jumped [this guy] and tore up my living room!

From that point forward, I started hauling equipment for the Monsters. I'd often have The Cult Heroes open for them too. Rock wasn't doing too much back then, but he [later] started doing the Sonic's Rendezvous Band with Fred Smith."

Mike Davis remembers the idea of working with Ron as an attractive prospect. "I thought that the combination of his ability and my ability in a band would just be fucking great. The hook up was the mating of The Stooges and the MC5. I would bring this kind of aggressive, big sound to the table and Ron would bring that Stooges simplicity. I just thought it'd be totally rocking. I saw all kinds of potential for it."

Niagara recalls some clash of egos between Ron Asheton and former MC5 man Mike Davis, but she didn't feel involved in that. "I was the girl so I wasn't afraid of anything. I wanted to sing in a band but I was nervous about doing an oral book report. I was looking forward to someone like Patti Smith picking up the gauntlet, but it wasn't what I expected. Debbie Harry was around and she was all girly, which was fine for her but I wanted to see someone more shocking, strong and masculine. I thought I had to do it. Now, everyone's in a band. Back then, everyone wasn't. But who wants to see a girl singer? I hate girl singers. What could be worse? It's always embarrassing. I remember every basement we played in. We didn't have a regular gig."

Describing Destroy All Monsters' sound, Niagara says that: "It was hardcore, it was high energy ... It was just hardcore music. At that time, everything was new wave. The first band was a new idea, so I was going backwards in a way. But I loved the MC5 and The Stooges. They were playing straight and I was the weird one. I was the girl singer, and like I said before, who the hell wants to hear that?"

Mike Davis: "There were a lot of people in the band, to begin with. There was the saxophone player, there were three guitarists – there was Ron, Larry Miller and Cary Loren. At first, it was pretty much all Cary Loren's musical ideas, which I thought were cool. He had a really raw approach to writing music. It wasn't an orthodox rock 'n' roll thing. It was kinda spacey, it was good. I liked it. We started to practise, but we were playing Cary's stuff really. We were feeling each other out to see what sound we were gonna have. At first it was really chaotic, but I really had high hopes for it, with Ron and I together in a band. I hoped it would turn out to be the best of the 5 and the best of The Stooges. Actually, if you listen to the stuff that we did towards the end of the band, it kind of has that feeling. It's pretty aggressive and experimental but it also has that pop approach to it. I don't think in either case, The Stooges or MC5, it was the epitome of anything, but it was representative and we wrote some really good songs."

Niagara and the Colonel both recall the fact that *Creem*'s Lester Bangs was a Destroy All Monsters Fan. Niagara: "Lester Bangs was here with *Creem* when we had something going on in Detroit. I didn't know him here, I met him in New York. He called me up though one day. It was early in the morning and I don't know why I answered the phone. He goes, 'Hi, I'm Lester Bangs and I've been listening all night to 'Bored'. It's so great, it sums it up.' He went on and on. First I was like, *Oh God it's Lester Bangs*. But then he went on. It was so bad because he was so drunk, he'd been listening to it all night. He was a great writer, no doubt, but it was just horrifyingly bad. I was just like, *Oh God, when can I get off the phone?* But I loved Lester. He loved to laugh, and he thought I was the funniest person he'd met. We had such a great time in New York, he was a riot. I just died when he died that young, it was horrifying."

Colonel: "He died wearing a Destroy All Monsters t-shirt."

Niagara: "What's weird is that I found out about his death second-hand, because I wasn't close enough for anyone to call me. I was so bummed. I was watching some show on the TV about The Beatles, and he came on. I was like, 'Oh it's Lester'. This was just a month later. He was wearing the Destroy All Monsters shirt on TV. That was some kind of something."

Friend of the band Shaun Claydon Carroll met Ron Asheton in 1978. "Ron was in Destroy All Monsters and Scott was drumming for Sonic's Rendezvous Band. There used to be a nightclub called Second Chance where both bands played at, and I went there around '77. I ended up working there from '78 to '82 because I was there all the time. I worked in the kitchen. There was a restaurant which closed at 9pm, and then the other side opened up and it was a nightclub.

I'm from London. We moved here when I was nine in 1969, and we moved to Ann Arbor, Michigan, in 1976 when I was 16. I graduated from high school and just stayed on. I loved Destroy All Monsters. It was loud guitar music. I liked them a lot. I still see Niagara every now and then. She's still in Detroit and she goes to shows."

Destroy All Monsters would embark on one UK tour that, though chaotic, would leave them fondly remembered in Britain. Niagara: "It was really fun and a lot of it was really intense because we were really pissed at DB, our manager who booked us. He booked it with this agency that was really small, and made a gentlemen's agreement on the phone. Then some other agency wanted to take care of us, and they were a nice agency. They would have actually made posters for us and promoted us. We found that out later. DB could have switched because he didn't even sign papers but he felt obliged after agreeing on the phone. We screwed up a little bit. But we still played for about a month and got lots of press. It was the first time in Europe so this place seemed romantically old, creepy and wonderful. I was like Alice In Wonderland. Our band was used to anything bad so we were just having a good time with everything. We were laughing about the food and the Scotch eggs – what the hell? Back then, it wasn't like you could get normal food either. It was all sausages and grease. We recovered from that after a while and went back to work. I couldn't believe all the people that took us seriously. People didn't go to Europe from Detroit. I didn't know anyone else that had done it. It was great to get it together, and it wasn't too horrible, now that it's over.

Mostly, the schedule was like, Ronnie would wake up in the afternoon. He'd scrounge for some food and stay in bed all day, then it'd be like 7.00 and we'd get ready. Ronnie sleeps really good. I remember taking pictures of Ronnie in bed, but not seeing any of the city we were in! I have a camera, and I'm taking pictures of Ronnie sleeping in every room. And he always sleeps with this little pillow on his head. I have all these cute pictures. My schedule never got right there. It was so loud, I'd fall asleep right in the room. We went around and did a lot of interviews and photo shoots. It was terribly charming. I liked it a lot."

Colonel: "The best bit of that is having to spend three days on standby at Heathrow airport. Can you imagine that? You know what it's like when your flight's delayed a couple of hours? Can you imagine how rock 'n' roll three days is? Finally, all of the workers at the airport chipped in to get them on a plane back home. The promoters thought there'd be more money in that tour. It was right when Lena Lovich came out and changed her little niche, blurring the lines into new wave. The timing was all wrong. Destroy All Monsters was a great band. It had the innocence, but it also had that crude punk sound. As soon as you started listening to it, you go, 'Yeah, that's the sound.' It really stands up today. When they try to recreate those film noir movies of the 1940s, they can't do it. You can't create those early punk beginnings again, like The Clash and The Sex Pistols. Something changes and you can't go back to that, but we managed to capture some of it with the box set. In [Destroy All Monsters off-shoot band] Dark Carnival, we tried to recapture that. I recorded every show for about six years, and there was only one or two shows that I was proud of and put on the box set."

Mike Davis: "There were only maybe half a dozen shows. I remember, right after the first show at Dingwalls, feeling really dispirited because it didn't go over with the kind of success that I was hoping for. I was hoping we'd blow the audience away, but it didn't happen that way. That was disappointing actually. The rest of the shows we played were as mediocre as the Dingwalls show. I remember that I felt pretty isolated from the band, if you could call it a band, because Ron and Niagara were just holed up in their room. We never really hung out much."

Though they are in short supply, Niagara is understandably proud of the studio recordings that the Monsters made. "Sometimes I'll hear them once in a while, and I'll think they sound really great. I think they came out decent. I'm trying to think what I hated about them, but all my complaints frittered away over the years. So much has happened since then. More's happening instead of less, I don't like to dwell a lot. That's why I'm glad I have a diary."

Still, she doesn't feel that the band ended before its time. "It went on for quite a while – almost eight years. That was a long time. I can't even believe it. It should have gone out a lot sooner than that. Sometimes we were playing a lot and sometimes not so much. Little by little we realised that we didn't care and we were burned out on the band. Everyone had that idea at once. We were just about able to pay rent in Ann Arbor. We lived with our roadie and his girlfriend.

I was with [Ronnie] until after the band, and we were trying to figure what we were gonna do. We had apartments but we were living off and on at his mother's house. It was incredibly odd. I called it the Asheton Farm. At different times, Kathy and Scotty would be living there too. Ann was amazing to put up with all that. She was a workaholic. She'd be washing and cooking all the time, basically for artists … I helped out a lot, but she wasn't gonna ask me … We were in a small room for years, and had a great time. We always liked when practise was cancelled, but when we did go it was great to hang out with the guys. It was hysterical. We used to go to the Star Lounge to see some cool punk bands, and they all loved Ronnie's playing. This was back when there were thirty people in bands and he was an idol of theirs. I remember Scotty reading me a dinosaur kids book and mispronouncing all the names. It was so funny. Most people wouldn't know about Scotty's sense of humour. He's pretty static. He'd loosen up at night when we'd all have drinks and get along."

Colonel: "The reverence that Destroy All Monsters carries in Tokyo is ridiculous. People are following Niagara wearing Destroy All Monsters shirts."

Niagara: "I didn't want to go to Japan but it was so great. Except I was scared to take my drugs but I should've because they didn't even know. Anyway, you go into one of the stores and they're all beautifully done. Black chandeliers, clear glass, stuff everywhere. They had pictures on the wall of Anita Pallenburg, Marianne

Faithful and me. I was like, this is a planet where this makes sense to me! That wouldn't happen in many places. It was almost too much for us."

Ron had certainly found musicians that he was comfortable with, because when Destroy All Monsters started to fizzle out, he stuck with Niagara in Colonel Galaxy's brainchild, Dark Carnival. Niagara: "Colonel saw us play as Destroy All Monsters. We were still playing here and there. Colonel called and he wanted to put a band together with all the weirdos! Somebody had suggested getting me and he thought it'd be impossible. He was putting on a show on New Years Eve, so he called me at 4.00 or 5.00 at night. I was yelling, 'Who would call this early? What are you, nuts?' The bottom line was that I'd make $100 for one night, so I agreed to do it. That was 1985. I played with Dark Carnival, and we might have had a couple of other gigs. We just gave it up in the end. I stopped playing, there'd be another Dark Carnival show so I'd do that, and then I started hanging out with Colonel a lot and ended up marrying him in 1986. I just wanted Ronnie to be friends with Colonel 'cos it was easier and better for him to do that. We were still getting along great, but it was like a brother and sister thing. I never got mad at him. He hung out with us, and … so I said 'Why don't you play?'"

Ron Asheton: "Destroy All Monsters was gone. Niagara and Colonel Galaxy put together an all-star revue. It'd be all the best guys. It'd be a switch off. I wouldn't have to do the whole set. They'd even switch drummers. It was the same deal, *OK, it's time for me to play music again.* So we did the same as Destroy All Monsters, but not as many shows. We tried to make it go to better places. Less shows, but trying to get a record deal. Scotty played, but for a very short time. Not as a regular. We got LJ Steel as a regular drummer. He was the best-known drummer from The Cult Heroes. Those guys are legends in this town. Party dudes … LJ went down to Georgia and got a really good job being a grip in movies. Then Niagara's artwork started taking off, during Dark

Carnival or even before. She was establishing herself and being successful. So it wasn't a bad death, it just laid down and went to sleep. It was cool. Everyone still cared about each other. It wasn't a 'fuck you' sort of break up. It was a good death."

The bass player for much of Dark Carnival's existence was Pete Bankert. "I worked with Ron and Scott Asheton, but never Iggy, I worked with them together and separately. With Ron, I played bass in Dark Carnival. We recorded *The Last Great Ride* at my studio in down river Detroit at the time. Don Flemming, a producer from Sonic Youth and a number of other projects, produced on it. Ron recorded a song for a punk compilation with Wayne Kramer at my studio, a song called 'Dead End Street' for an album called *Beyond Cyberpunk*. That's pretty much what I did. Larry played drums for Dark Carnival, but I think Ron pretty much played guitar, bass and sang. I recorded two Scott Morgan Band albums with Scott Asheton playing drums. Scott and I played in a band called The Farleys, which was pretty much a studio band. We released stuff on our own website – we didn't have a label or anything. I recorded Scott on a couple of Sonny Vincent records. One was called *Paralex In Wonderland*. The one after, I forget what it was called. Sonny Vincent's put out a whole bunch of records, but I only did the two that Scott Asheton played on. He's a European artist, more or less. I think he was living in Germany.

Ron and Scott are a lot different. Ron's a lot more reserved, stays to himself. He's a straight up guy. Scott has a wife and a kid, and he's a little more outgoing, I'd guess you'd say. Scott's wife and my ex-girlfriend were best of friends. We lived by each other. I guess I worked with both of them quite a lot. It's kind of hard to get to know Ron, but once you do get to know him, he's as down-to-earth as you could be. I partied more with Scott.

I recorded some of the early incarnations of the Carnival. They were like one-off shows they recorded with a cast of people. A bunch of different singers would come up and sing their song that they were known for. At some point, they had to solidify a band because they toured Australia, and that's when I joined the band. We did a couple of New York stints.

Niagara's an artist. Before Ron got in the band, [DAM] was like an art-noise project. Once Ron got in, it got more like a rock band and she turned into a punk rock girl. She was perfect for that. She really represented that. Her voice! She's a good frontwoman. Music, painting – she's been in the arts a long time. Ron was a professional. He doesn't come in all fucked up on liquor and drugs. He prepares for his recording like a professional."

Friends of the Ashetons, Shaun Claydon Carroll told the author: "I liked Ron's guitar, but I didn't find Dark Carnival as interesting. It wasn't as intense. Destroy All Monsters was exciting, and you never really knew what was going to happen. It was totally unpredictable from show to show."

One of Ron's best friends was Billy Cheatham, who died about ten years ago. Bill has two daughters, and every Christmas Ron has this small Christmas party, and Bill's daughters come over. Ron is Uncle Ron to them. They know he was in The Stooges and they see him now The Stooges have got back together. He's just their Uncle Ron, he makes sure they get Christmas presents and have a good time at Christmas. That's sort of a different side to him to what people see. Ron is totally not a wild man."

Niagara: "DAM was definitely punky and hardcore. I thought it was funny. That was high energy, intense and hardcore. Dark Carnival was also hardcore, but we did more slower, melodic things. It was kinda deathly romantic things. It's more moody. It took me and Ronnie years to get this great system for writing together. I was realising that Ronnie would play something and I would try to work with him on it, and he'd get touchy if anyone was around. What sounded best was him playing these melodic, romantic things. We had a lot of fun doing Dark Carnival. Ronnie's an emotional player. Ronnie was in this movie with

Thurston Moore, *Velvet Goldmine* and ... Thurston was saying that Ronnie should only write ballads. Sad songs are his forte."

With Dark Carnival over, Niagara is concentrating on her art from her home in Michigan where she lives with the Colonel. "Dark Carnival probably lasted longer than it should have done. I wanted to go back to art. I was pretty young, and you go to a gallery and they treat you like shit, even now. If I got a grey wig, it'd really help. Now, I can get anywhere. But if nobody knew me, I'd wear a grey wig. It's the older you are in the art business. When we'd play a club, I would do the walls and get money for that. I put together a show with paintings. I did a huge window display in Royal Oak. I couldn't get in a gallery, so I thought I could have them on site for 24 hours a day instead on 9-5 anyway, and then they all sold. That was a surprise to everybody, because you never know what anybody will buy. Just selling that shop gave me more money than I'd made my *whole career* in music. I wasn't even thinking of the money, you just do what you can do. I started painting more, and [then] someone opened a gallery in the early 1990s. That was a good gallery, showing *Juxtapose* magazine type stuff. Since then, I've been travelling around the world doing art shows and doing good. They want me to play here and there and I can do that. In Tokyo, I played with a Japanese band and they knew everything perfect. Everything there is perfect. These people love to work, they're so impressive.

What I'm liking more is staying in my so called den and just paint and do creative stuff on my own. Drugs help me with that, and many other things. I miss seeing people though, all the artists I met. I like to go around Europe once in a while."

Following Dark Carnival's eventual conclusion, the band's bassist Pete Bankert played with Scott Asheton in the punk rock band The Farleys. "We did an entire CD of Stooges covers, and we did an original CD of their songs. We were hired guns. This was about four or five years ago, just before The Stooges got back together [in 2003]. Scott was making pocket money. I told them that if they hired Scott and paid me as a studio engineer, I would play for free. They got a deal on it." Bankert can now be found in the Detroit band Send More Cops.

While Ron was mashing with the Monsters and playing at the Carnival, Scott Asheton had hooked up with MC5 guitarist Fred Smith in the Sonic's Rendezvous Band. The singer of that band was former Rationals man Scott Morgan: "Well, Fred and I met through the MC5. The first guy [from the MC5] I met really was Wayne [Kramer], when I went to see them around '66 ... and Fred was the quiet one of the band, so I didn't talk to him much. And as I got to know them, I talked to him a little bit more, but he was pretty much the quiet one.

Scott Asheton and I knew each other, and Gary Rasmussen also, through the same circles, and so when Fred and I needed a drummer for Sonic's Rendezvous Band, I suggested Scott and he got involved as the drummer in 1975. Then we needed a bass player after that and Scott and I had been hanging around with Gary, so we told Fred that Gary's our man and he joined the band and it just stuck. So that was '76, and that was the [line-up] that did most of the Sonic's Rendezvous Band stuff."

Before Rasmussen, Ron Cooke, the bass player in Mitch Ryder's Detroit, had been on four string duties. "I left the Sonic's Rendezvous Band because I'd had enough of it. When the story's told, I'm included in it and that's all I wanted.

We started rehearsing and writing songs together, and Scott and I became best friends. We started hanging out together all the time. Before that, we weren't really that close. We were more like acquaintances who both played music in the same town.

I do wish we had done more recordings. It's funny that all of the Ann Arbor bands have some strange little quirk to their story, and that's the Sonic's Rendezvous Band one. We could never agree on a proper deal with a record company to release an album. We had plenty of material, as you can see from the box set [released on Easy Action Records]. There's sixty-something different tracks there. Certainly more than one album's worth of stuff. It is kinda ironic that we didn't release any albums at the time. We only put out that one song ['City Slang']. It just happened that way. We didn't plan it. But then you look back, it's kinda like the most unique story you could come up with. A band that are together for six years and are pretty good and they only release one song! It's kinda weird.

One night we were sitting in the car in the Asheton's driveway, and Fred was talking about how strong Arnold Schwarzenegger was. I said, 'He's not strong. Scott's stronger than him.' The next thing I know, Fred's doing this whole thing on stage, which is on the box set. He says, 'He ain't got no sissy weights, he uses sticks to beat'. Stuff like that. His nickname was The Grim Beater."

As mentioned, when Ron Cooke felt like he'd had enough, former The Up man Gary Rasmussen filled his boots. "I believe I was the direct choice. I'd known everybody for a long time before that, so I think I was the natural choice. The Stooges and The Up were managed by the same people, we had the same booking agent, and we played basically the same gigs. I knew everybody – I knew Fred, and it just seemed like a natural thing. [Scott Asheton and I] always got along fine. Scott's just the way he is. Even as a drummer. If someone asked him to play a drum fill and put a big roll in there, he'd kinda go 'no'. He's kinda different to most drummers. He'd rather just be solid. Bashing away back there instead of playing a bunch of frilly junk. We hung out together all the time. Rock wasn't a big talker, just a good guy to hang around with. With Rock, we'd just talk about who had the beer stash! And he's still that way. He's never gonna call me up and have long, in-depth business calls."

Despite the lack of Sonic's Rendezvous Band studio recordings, Rasmussen is understandably proud of the music he made with

Scott Asheton, and the strong rhythm section that they forged together. "Everyone has their own thing. It's not a matter of better or worse. There are a lot of people I liked playing with. As a bass player, I just had to listen to their style. When you're playing bass, you're playing what the drummer is playing, but you're also playing the notes that the guitar players are playing. My job is to link the two together, and keep the rhythm strong at the bottom so it all sounds right. If you don't have a good foundation, it doesn't matter what's going on up top.

I think the playing was fine. Sometimes I wish we went to the studio more, or at all. A lot of the recordings are live that somebody recorded with a cassette recorder and a couple of mics in the room. It's not the most hi-fidelity, but I can hear everything and I don't have a problem with the playing."

The Sonic's band, with their anthem 'City Slang', made waves across Detroit, but would implode before recording an album. Still, their career has been neatly compiled by Easy Action Records in the Sonic's Rendezvous Band box set.

Following the break-up of the Sonic's Rendezvous Band, Scott Asheton continued to work with Scott Morgan in The Scott Morgan Band, and later in Scott's Pirates, also with Gary Rasmussen, who put out a self-titled album.

Scott Morgan: "They kept the Sonic's band together at first. Scott, Gary and Fred tried to keep the band together after I [left]. But all they did was go to the studio and record a few basic instrumental tracks. They never finished them. They just kinda hung out socially, but nothing really happened after that."

Iggy Pop admits that he didn't pay much attention to what his former band mates were doing. "I was dimly aware of the thing Ron did with Niagara. That was a head scratcher for me. There was something that he was trying to put together on the West Coast that wasn't going so well. I think Dennis Thompson talked about it in *Sonically Speaking*. I still don't know much about that. I think one of those bands had the visual artist Mike Kelly. That's kinda interesting. Scott, I always [checked out] anything Fred Smith did. Fred, to me, was the spine of the MC5 musically, and was a real legendary musician in a certain way. So the Rendezvous band I was aware of. 'Sister Anne' I thought was a good piece of writing. 'City Slang' and some of Fred's later writing — you can really see that he was going in a certain direction. But they never put out much stuff. I think I saw them play one night in a bar and I think I might have sang a song with them. I just remember that it was a good, solid, heartfelt band that summed up everything that an idealistic Mid-West kid would think a rock band should be. With that mysterious maddening twist that Fred had, because he had a withdrawn mystique about him. That's kinda what it was like playing with him."

In the 1990s, Scott Asheton would work with Sonny Vincent, formerly of proto-punks The Testors. Something of an underground punk icon himself, Vincent would put out two records with Asheton behind the kit, including 1993's *Roller Coaster*. Asheton would also tour extensively with Vincent.

More recently, he played with The Farleys just prior to The Stooges' [2003] reformation. The Farleys were formed in 1996 by brothers Mike and Mark Mitchell. Scott Asheton, plus Pete Bankert, hooked up with the band in 2000 and recorded two albums — *Youth In Asia* and *Meet The Stooges*, the latter a CD exclusively consisting of Stooges songs, although some of them were given a Farleys makeover. 'Death Trip', for example, was re-worked as 'Bus Trip'. Primal and rough.

HENRY FORD – A DAY AT A MUSEUM

On one of my quieter days in Detroit, when I was kind of at a loose end and looking for something to do, it came to my attention that The Henry Ford Museum was hosting an exhibition entitled 'Rock Stars' Cars & Guitars'. Fairly self-explanatory, this was to be a display of vehicles and guitars owned by various famous musicians. I made my way over there for two reasons. The first is that I'm always happy to look at guitars, especially those belonging to respected musicians. The second is that, in all honesty, any book that has Detroit as its location has to touch upon the motor industry. It is, after all, the motor city. True enough, it's impossible to get a real picture of the factory industry and the working man's life while walking through a museum. But still, some knowledge of Ford's rich history was never going to hurt.

The guitars were mildly distracting but not fascinating. Most of them were from the private collection of Cheap Trick man Rick Nielsen, and there were Kiss, ZZ Top and Alice Cooper axes to look through too. The cars were more interesting – Kiss's recording studio trailer was amazing, as was Marilyn Manson's 'death Lincoln'. But, perhaps surprisingly, the main part of the museum was equally as appealing. The Wiener Mobile has to be seen to be believed, but just walking through the Ford cars as they took shape over the years, imagining the hours of panel beating and spray painting done by the average Detroiter was fairly humbling. This is a city that, in its heyday, was right in the centre of the motor industry boom, and it has every right to be proud.

My other Ford-related excursion was to the Ford Field to see the Detroit Lions play football (that's American football, folks). They were playing the Minnesota Vikings and the game was sold out, but I managed to pick up a ticket from a dodgy looking character outside for $40. It was a great seat too, and an extraordinary game. I had never seen American football live before, but I had liked it for a long time. I had been to see the Red Wings play (ice hockey) against Phoenix during my MC5 trip, but this was *something completely different. The Lions, you see, are not a good team. They've been bad for years, and yet the people of Detroit show up week after week to cheer them on. This is testament to the spirit of the place and, though not exclusive to Detroit, it's further proof of their never-say-die attitude. After the fourth quarter, the game was tied at fourteen each. The game went into overtime (an extra 15 minutes of play, with the first team to go ahead winning the game), after the Vikings had hit the upright post with a 52-yard field goal attempt. That Minnesota were millimetres away from winning the game just added to the drama, and when the Lions successfully kicked a field goal in overtime and won the game, the place erupted. The walk back to the car amongst the crowd was a special one. "It's like we've won the Superbowl!" said one guy walking near me, and he was right. A Lions victory is so rare that the town really celebrates whenever they get the opportunity.*

A week later, and I was at Comerica Park to watch the Detroit Tigers (baseball) play the Minnesota Twins (yep, Minnesota again), along with Danielle from Crud. Again, Detroit won, although it was far less dramatic. They won with a shut out – an 8-0 victory that showed just how dominant the Tigers were in the game. The Tigers made the play-offs the year before, but this year they just missed out. Still, they're a great team and another reason for the city to be proud. As if they needed one.

CHAPTER 7

Iggy Pop's post-Stooges career has been well documented in countless tomes dedicated to the man, but a book about The Stooges would be missing something without even an overview of the man's career.

While meeting with Detroit legend Russ Gibb, he said to me that, "Iggy invented the stage dive, as far as I know. I'd never heard of anybody doing it before him. Maybe one day he'll receive an award for it."

Uncle Russ may have a point, but Iggy's solo career offered up plenty of great music as well as acrobatics. The Stooges, much like the MC5, came to an end with no big fanfare, no tearful farewell. They just ended. There was a limbo period though, when Iggy and James Williamson worked together on a record called *Kill City*. Williamson: "I think it could have been a very good album. We were never able to progress it far enough to make it what it should have been. Some of the material came from the previous Stooges tour.

By that time, I had pretty much had enough of the music business. As I had been involved in making albums and so on, the studio process had intrigued me. More and more, I got interested in that and thought, *Maybe this is what I'll do instead of killing myself as a rock 'n' roll guitar player. Maybe I'll work in a studio.* But once I got started doing that, I soon got more fascinated by the emergence of the personal computer which was just beginning at that point. I mean, you wouldn't even recognise it today. It had switches on the front panel and some really basic things you had to do. But nonetheless, it was cool what you could do, compared to other things in those days. So I got fascinated by that and started to study that, and eventually ended up being an electrical engineer and moving to the Silicon Valley. The rest is history."

Without a band behind him, Iggy felt creatively free and he retreated to Paris with *Raw Power* collaborator David Bowie to record *The Idiot*. In *Strange Fascination*, his biography of David Bowie, David Buckley would write: "Bowie and Iggy worked through July on the album in France, then relocated first to the Musicland Studios in Munich and finally to the Hansa Studios, Berlin, to complete the work.

Iggy Pop is a man of incredible extremes. According to one Bowie fan's testimony, one minute he would barge straight through someone walking arm-in-arm down a corridor with a band member of a Bowie tour, or scream 'Burn me, burn me!' through a hotel lobby if he saw someone smoking. The next, he was your regular, friendly, weird guy … One thing for certain is that he has one of the most distinctive voices in pop history. Low, crunching, gnarled, wrecked, it reached bottomless pits of anguish in just one syllable. *The Idiot*, viewed from the perspective of a quarter of a century later, now sounds closer to the sound Bowie was perfecting on his own 'White Light' tour than *Low* itself does. It's a funky, robotic hell-hole of an album, full of droll conceits and great melodies."

Happy with the way his creative partnership with Bowie had gone, Iggy stuck with his friend for his second solo effort, *Lust For Life*. A far more upbeat and energetic record, the title track would become Iggy's best known and most loved solo song. In *Loving The Alien*, his biography of Bowie, Christopher Sandford wrote that, "In rapid succession, Bowie helped to write, arrange and produce Iggy's follow up to *The Idiot*. Astonishingly, this prototype of the wasted punk now became a health addict. He and Bowie regularly cycled or walked the Hauptstrasse to the Hansa Studio and Iggy took up weight lifting. The results not only showed in *Lust*'s grinning, full-face cover photograph, but inevitably fuelled the music. Full of lithe, upbeat songs and lyrics that celebrated sex, the album was a top thirty hit in Britain and America."

It's the title track that opens the record, a swaggering bass line and Iggy sounding at his happiest. It's a great song, one that the movie *Trainspotting* would later transport into cinema history.

'The Passenger' is another of Iggy's best known tunes, and deservedly so, although it's not necessarily an obvious classic. The vocal delivery is typically monotone and though there's a 'la la' chorus, it barely shifts in pace or key. Still, it's deadpan genius and will forever be a fan's favourite.

With a few turkeys behind him, Iggy took a four-year break from the studio before reuniting with Bowie in 1986 for the *Blah Blah Blah* record. While not the glorious comeback it could have been, the album was still something of a return to form. Opening with a raucous version of Australian rock 'n' roller Johnny O'Keefe's 1950s hit 'Real Wild Child', *Blah Blah Blah* is as polished as anything Iggy has ever put out, an attempt to appeal to a wider market. Even an appearance by Sex Pistol Steve Jones on 'Cry For Love' couldn't add an edge to what is essentially an MOR album. Still, the songs are stronger than anything Iggy had put his name to since *Lust For Life*, and his career appeared to back on track.

Of course, there are few artists more self-destructive than Iggy, and he would follow up *Blah Blah Blah* with the far inferior *Instinct*. An attempt to get back to his rawer roots, the motives behind the record were sound. Unfortunately, the songs are so dull that, once again, not even the fact that he was collaborating with Steve Jones could save the album. The front cover portrait and the sub-glam metal fonts used for Iggy's name and the album title do little to improve matters.

Next up was *Brick By Brick*, produced by Was (Not Was) man Don Was, and really the album that Iggy fans had been patiently waiting for. Bringing in Guns N' Roses (now Velvet Revolver) men Slash and Duff McKagen on guitar and bass respectively for the songs 'Home', 'Butt Town', 'Pussy Power' and 'My Baby Wants To Rock And Roll', the record was gifted with a heavier edge and, together with the quality of the songs, it made for something of a gem. When the history of rock is written, *Brick By Brick* is often forgotten. But for those of us who needed a great Iggy album, it's a mainstay on the stereo.

American Caesar kept the ball rolling, packed with great songs and guests like former Black Flag man Henry Rollins, and then Iggy took another stumble with the truly abysmal *Naughty Little Doggy*. 1999's *Avenue B* saw Iggy again working with Don Was on what was a departure for the singer. Having recently broken up with his girlfriend Alejandra, Iggy saw fit to pour his heartache and anger into a record that is a very hit and miss affair. When it works, like on 'Nazi Girlfriend', it works well. But all too often the album veers too close to 'dull' and it's very definitely not a rock record. While true fans applauded his courage and desire to stretch himself, sales were poor.

While widely derided, many fans saw 2001's *Beat Em Up* as the perfect Iggy record, full of driving riffs and angry vocals, and some great tunes too. Long time guitarist Whitey Kirst stuck around, and was complemented in the band now known as 'The Trolls' by his brother and former Nymphs man Alex Kirst. Bodycount bassist Mooseman was brought in on bass (Mooseman was tragically killed in front of a hardware store in February 2001, the victim of a random shooting). The main criticism aimed at *Beat Em Up* was that it was 'boneheaded rock', something that it's difficult to argue with when listening to songs like 'The Jerk' and 'It's All Sh*t'. But with Iggy taking the bull by the horns once again, it was difficult not to get dragged along for the ride.

As well as his own albums, Iggy has contributed to many soundtracks and other people's records over the years. In 1984, he appeared on the main theme to the movie *Repo Man*, and three years later he contributed the track 'Risky' to the Ryuichi Sakamoto movie *Neo Geo*. Goth rockers The Cult benefited from Iggy's backing vocals on 'New York City' from their 1989 album *Sonic Temple*, and he dueted with Blondie's Debbie Harry on 'Well, Did You Evah!' for the *Red, White And Blue* compilation album in 1990. He hooked up with Detroit homeboys Was (Not Was) on there are *You OK?* album for the song 'Elvis's Rolls Royce', and with psychobilly punks The Cramps on their *Look Mom No Head* album for the song 'Miniskirt Blues'. The latter song features Iggy and Cramps frontman Lux Interior trading vocals and having a great time doing it. The Cramps' shock rock imagery and horror movie lyrics were a perfect fit for Iggy and, ironically, it's one of the better songs he appeared on during the early part of the 1990s. Also of note, he appeared on the song 'Black Sunshine' from the *La Sexorcisto: Devil Music Vol. 1* album by B-movie metallers White Zombie, and in 1999 he hooked up with experimental dance band Death In Vegas for the track 'Aisha' from their *The Contino Sessions* record. Perhaps his finest moment as a guest vocalist came when he joined up with short lived avant-garde art rockers At The Drive In. Singing 'Rolodex Propaganda' from the classic *Relationship Of Command* album, Iggy brilliantly sold himself to a whole new audience.

He also joined up with foul-mouthed female rapper Peaches for the song 'Kick It' from her 2003 *Father Fucker* album. Peaches would later return the favour, performing with Iggy on his *Skull Ring* record.

GUSOLINE ALLEY AND JIMMY DOOM

*In the suburb of Royal Oak, very close to the Royal Oak Theatre, sits a
bar called Gusoline Alley. While researching The Stooges, Gus's became my
favourite bar in Detroit and it's surrounding area for a variety of reasons.
It has the best jukebox ever. Seriously, EVER! The beer selection has to
be admired. It's always busy, and the vibe in the place is always great.*

*Jimmy Doom is the singer in a punk band called The Almighty
Lumberjacks of Death. Yes, really. He's also a very good stand up comedian
in the Bill Hicks/Henry Rollins mould, and Jerry Vile's* Orbit *magazine
once printed a nude picture of him lying across Gus's bar. It wasn't a pretty
picture! But Jimmy Doom is one of those guys that is just full of stories,
and when he heard about my Stooges project he contacted me through a
friend to tell me these little gems. Enjoy.*

"I don't have the year but I guess it was about '88. A local rock radio
station, rarely played Iggy, when Iggy made that comeback. It was a $30
ticket, which back in those days was amazingly high. They did this big
promotion where they gave away buttons which got you into the show.
People called up and got these buttons, which were about 1.5" in diameter.
They gave away about 120 of them. The capacity of St Andrews is about
1200. People were scalping tickets and nobody was buying. People were
walking in. They didn't have any watermark on the button and it wasn't
numbered. The scalpers were thinking, 'Iggy's playing, we gonna make a
million dollars', while someone else who was a genius was bootlegging the
Iggy buttons and people were just walking into the show. Before Iggy goes
on, people who actually purchased tickets couldn't get in because there were
so many people in there with the bootlegged buttons.

*Very recently, Iggy played in Memphis Tennessee at the Beale Street
Music Festival. It originated on Beale Street in Memphis but now it's a
huge Budweiser sponsored, 4-stage big festival. Iggy played a stage with
Jerry Lee Lewis and some others I don't remember because basically we*

149

were there to see Iggy. There's this restaurant, a barbeque. After the Iggy show, everybody just bails and goes down to the local bars. All of a sudden Iggy and like five guys walk into this place. Iggy orders the fucking ribs. They got the homemade barbeque sauce. They're kissing Iggy's ass, they know who the fuck he is. Iggy takes a slab of ribs, tears them apart, shoves the meat in his throat, and there's a million witnesses to this, takes the homemade barbeque sauce, and while he's chewing the shit, tilts his head back and pours the barbeque sauce into his throat! The next day and there's a rumour that Iggy has an Iggy-suit. [The theory is] that Iggy is totally dying, and that when you see him and he's so well built, it's because he wears a vinyl muscle suit to make it look like he's not dying! This is running through every bar in fucking Memphis. I'm like, 'Iggy's in good shape man' … and they're like, 'No, that's a vinyl Iggy suit.' That's not a suit, I saw him onstage sweating. Unless he bought a suit that sweats. My girlfriend and I were seven people deep from the front, and there's no way in fucking hell that he's sweating through a suit. Somebody's gotta run with that idea … somebody will one day pick up on it!

The old Detroit punk club Bookies reopened on 6 Mile. In the heyday, Iggy and those guys would play there on 6 Mile, just this little dive. This guy Phil resurrected it, and he went back to a gay club but he [then] started having punk nights. People would let their kids go, because they remembered going when they were a young punk. It was really seedy … you'd hear kids say, 'This is where The Stooges played' and I would say 'Like The Stooges are ever gonna show up here for any reason, they're done with that.' We're playing one night, my band The Almighty Lumberjacks of Death are playing. It's the same original stage that The Stooges played on, and at the end of the show I grabbed on a light truss that was no longer in use, it was just bolted to the ceiling, and I jumped into the crowd at the end of the set and I fucking roll off. Kids are going nuts, whatever, it's great! My buddy Keith is just pointing at this guy. I'm like, 'Is it a cop?' It was fucking Ron Asheton, and he walks up to me, shakes my hand and said, 'Jimmy, you guys were fucking great.' I'm like, 'Oh my God, a Stooge actually showed up here after they'd been closed for like a decade.'"

CHAPTER 8

As the 1990s approached, Ron Asheton turned to B-movie horror as an alternative career direction, with mixed results. In 1988, he starred as 'Peter' in a little production called The Carrier, in which the main character, Jake, is the carrier of a virus that affects every inanimate object that he touches. Then, when another person touches that object, they're dissolved into it. Not quite Pride & Prejudice then. 1992's Hellmaster was no better, although Ron Asheton's role was bigger, taking the part of Mama Jones. The story involved a crazy college professor who got his kicks by injecting students with a potion that transformed them into violent, zombie-like killers. If nothing else, Asheton seemed to be having fun with his roles.

1995 saw the release of *Mosquito*, a movie that saw Asheton's character Hendricks The Park Ranger alongside Gunnar Hansen (from *Texas Chainsaw Massacre*) who played Earl The Bank Robber in a story that involved mosquitoes growing to the size of a large bird after feeding on the corpses of aliens that have crashed in a swamp. I kid you not.

But Asheton wasn't even close to done. He played the role of 'Russell' in 1995's *Legion Of The Night*, in which a scientist creates zombie killing machines for an organised crime boss but, predictably, the said zombies escape, creating carnage in the city.

In 1996, Asheton starred in his last movie (for the time being?), imaginatively entitled *Frostbiter: Wrath Of The Wendigo*. Ron played 'Gary' while Scott Asheton made a cameo appearance as 'guy at the bar'. The story involves a beast (the Wendigo) which is set free when some redneck hunters break a sacred circle. The beast then kills people, until it's stopped.

Ron Asheton: "That started when I was still in Destroy All Monsters. The first picture I did was around '85. Ironically enough, it was LJ Steel and his girlfriend who were gonna audition for this picture [*The Carrier*] and they go 'come with us'. I love movies. I wanted to be an actor since I was a kid. So I go, 'OK, I'll go.' They say 'read for a part.' So I got in line and I waited, and I made the cut. I made the first cut, then the second. LJ and his girlfriend made the second cut but they didn't make it past that. He did it for fun. I made the final four and I was waiting for that phone call. They call and say, 'You got your part.' Yay. So for me, it was a dream come true. It was a quirky, weird movie. I thought the script was kinda neat and weird … it was just when AIDS was happening. If it would have happened a little bit later, it would have been more forceful. It wound up being a $600,000 movie. It was the first time in years I'd had all my hair cut off. The movie took place in the 1950s, so I had it cut. I actually thought it was pretty cool. I got so into it that I kept that hairstyle for a little bit longer. Slicked back. Everyone started calling me 'Dad'. 'You look like someone's dad.' But it was fun being in the movie, and that got the movie bug going for me. I auditioned for a lot of pictures. I got in *Let's Kill All The Lawyers*. I had a small part in that, which was cool. Of course, that movie didn't even make it to cassette. For *Hellmaster: Soulstealer* with John Saxon, I played his wife, an evil nun. I actually went just to help. They asked me if I'd help audition actors, because I have a good eye for it. There was really no part for me, just a small group of a woman and two bad guys. I had fun doing it, and then the director goes, 'What can we do for you?' I go, 'Well, you can't. I don't wanna work as a crew guy because I have no expertise in anything that would be other than me being a PA, being a gopher running around doing shit I don't wanna do.' He goes, 'Well, I can find something.' He gets back to me and goes, 'How would you like to be Mama Jones?' I go, 'What? That's a woman's part.' He goes, 'We could not find a woman that would be tough enough for that part.' So it was awesome. I had really cool special effects make up. It took a couple of hours to put on. I went to a tailor and had a perfect nun's habit made for me. I had a great time doing that.

I kept going onto other roles. Probably the one that's actually still seen today on TV is *Mosquito*. I got the movie bug so bad, and that was one of the things that helped kill Destroy All Monsters. Niagara was pissed that I gave too much time to the movies. That was one of the reasons that the band broke up – she kinda broke up with me. I love this movie thing, but I'm trying to crack a nut that's even harder than what I'm already doing as a musician. What am I gonna do? Fucking go out to LA where there's 10,000 actors … I haven't given up on that. I got to do some music for *Mosquito* also. At the end of the picture, there's the big dramatic roll out, and I do the black and white roll out with a song I wrote with Pete Bankert and LJ Steel who were in Dark Carnival.

Now I'm friends with Gunner Hansen. Little did I know it was the movie to take a date to, because the girls would grab hold of you all scared. If you sit down with him, he's an imposing figure at 6' 4", 250lbs. He's from Iceland. But if you sit down with him, it's like being with a college professor of English. He's really an intelligent man. He enjoys the good Scotch and cigars like I do. We're good friends still."

While Ron was having fun with fake blood, Iggy was having a bit of a film career of his own. In 1986, he made a cameo in *Sid & Nancy*, the biopic of Sid Vicious of the Sex Pistols and his girlfriend Nancy Spungen. However, it was in 1990 that Iggy proved his big screen worth. John Waters had become a cult director thanks to underground movies like *Pink Flamingos* and *Hairspray*. *Crybaby* saw him with a bigger budget for a musical movie that had Johnny Depp in the lead role as Crybaby, a bad boy rock 'n' roller in love with a 'straight' girl. Like a punk rock *Grease*, *Crybaby* was funny and raw, and was the perfect vehicle for Iggy in his role as Depp's Uncle Belvedere Rickettes.

In 1995, he played the roll of Ratface in the much-maligned comic book adaptation *Tank Girl*, and then he continued the graphic novel theme when he played main bad guy Curve in *City Of Angels*, the sequel to the classic *The Crow*. Rather bizarrely, Iggy would also voice a new born baby in *Rugrats: The Movie* in 1998, a spin off from the successful cartoon series.

Iggy comes across best when he's playing himself though, something that he was able to do in *Coffee & Cigarettes*. A series of vignettes that all have coffee and cigarettes in common, Iggy stars in a segment entitled 'Somewhere In California' alongside Tom Waits. The two singers meet in a café and have a horribly awkward conversation. When Iggy tells Waits that he can call him Iggy, Waits replies, "Well, Jim ..." It's a great piece of film that sees two musical legends playing off of each other beautifully.

In 1998, the previously mentioned movie *Velvet Goldmine* came out, directed by Todd Haynes. The film was a thinly veiled recreation of the story of Iggy and Bowie's meeting and subsequent relationship. The role of the Iggy character (Curt Wild) was played by *Trainspotting* star Ewan McGregor, with the Bowie character (Brian Slade) played by Jonathan Rhys Meyers. The movie, though essentially fiction, toyed with the notion that there was a sexual aspect to the relationship between the two rock stars, with Haynes' use of colour and music creating an eminently watchable film. The reviews weren't all complimentary, but the film has become something of an underground favourite.

Interestingly, the soundtrack to the movie featured Ron Asheton. The guitarist had a fruitful time in the studio with Mudhoney man Mark Arm, though only the song 'My Unclean' would make the final cut (although, as mentioned, the movie band could also be heard performing The Stooges' track, 'TV Eye').

Ron Asheton: "That [was] some fun stuff. I met Don Flemming. He called me up. It was him, [Minuteman bassist] Mike Watt, Thurston Moore – Don did that Backbeat movie and had worked with Thurston so they were already tight. He was looking to put together a band that was like The Stooges. Thurston Moore goes 'Why don't you just call Ron Asheton?' It wound up being really cool. I did that first bit, then we went back and went back and recorded some songs, including 'TV Eye' and 'My Unclean'. But the best thing that came out of it was meeting and hanging out with Mike Watt. I've seen Thurston a few times but actually getting to know all those guys a lot better – we wound up doing The Wylde Ratttz record. It was gonna come out on London Records. How fucking cool – that Stones first 45. I was so excited, but as luck would have it, London Records got bought out and all the projects were shelved. I guess you can [hear] bits and pieces on the net. I have one CD and I haven't listened to it in a while because I don't wanna destroy it."

A DETROIT THING

Another stroke of luck smacked me around the head while I was researching this book. The Anthony Brancaleone film A Detroit Thing was receiving its premiere at the Detroit Film Theatre and I was going to be in town to attend the screening, plus the pre-show and after-show parties. Telling the story of the east side Detroit music scene over the past decade, the movie opens with the line "I'm not saying all of this is true, but this is how I remember it", narrated by Brancaleone, before showing a couple of hours of footage featuring some of Detroit's favourite underground rockers (and one – Kid Rock – who actually made the breakthrough to mainstream success). It's difficult to ignore the influence of The Stooges as bands like all girl group Stun Gun, gutter punks the Trash Brats, funk rockers The Howling Diablos and sleaze diva Queen Bee blast past on screen. Even Kid Rock appears to have borrowed some of Iggy's on-stage persona. The real story, however, is of the community that built around the east side scene. When Kid Rock gets signed, Tino from the Howling Diablos is visibly delighted for him despite his own recording contract being yet to appear, even to this day. This is a Detroit thing. I spoke to Brancaleone after the screening, to discuss the extent of The Stooges' influence on the bands that he had so lovingly filmed.

BC: When did you start making the film?
AB: "The movie was a seven year process, but having said that I used film footage from '96 to 2001 to tell the story.

BC: Did the film evolve as it went along?
AB: "When we began filming, Kid Rock wasn't signed by Atlantic Records yet. So I wanted to create a rock 'n' roll fairy tale. It was going to be a little less documentary and a little more fairy tale at the time. I figured if you were watching this movie in Miami or something, and you saw all these stadiums filled with people, people would wonder 'Are these bands

real or not? How are they shooting all this stuff?' I was kinda excited about that. When Kid Rock was signed to Atlantic, it took about six months before he really exploded. That kinda altered my story. I was working on a record at the time, and we stopped working on the film for almost two years. When we came back to it, I rewrote the story to be more of a true tale. It's a real life rock 'n' roll fairy tale now. It turned out to be what we wanted it to be."

BC: How did you decide which bands to include and which not to?
AB: "I'm of the opinion that we have endless musical talent in Detroit. You can go out and see a band on almost any night of the week and you're gonna have a pretty good time. We filmed 25-30 bands, and when I started editing the movie, I knew what I wanted my opening to be. Musically, I began with Robert Bradley, and it just flowed naturally one band to the next band."

BC: How much of an influence do you think The Stooges had on bands like the Trash Brats and Queen Bee?
AB: Ah, they influenced the whole scene of music here. The whole garage rock scene and even the rap scene – everybody knows the MC5 and The Stooges. There's a lot of bands from the Detroit area like that – Grand Funk Railroad. Kid Rock likes Nugent, Bob Seger, stuff like that. Iggy is technically from Ann Arbor, but we look at him as a Detroiter because he made his bones here. A lot of these bands would have been greatly influenced by The Stooges. In fact, all of punk rock music is greatly influenced by them."

BC: For a lot of people in attendance at the premiere, the movie was like watching a home movie. How do you think it'll do outside of Detroit?
AB: "I actually think it'll do better outside of Detroit. Most of the comments I get from people who aren't really into that scene say that they get a full story. I'm really looking forward to getting it out of Detroit. I'm glad we had a good turn out for the screening, but like you said, this is

their life so they looked at it in a way to see themselves on film. They recognise everything. I think they're looking at the movie almost too literally. They need to stand back and see it for what it is. It's just a good story and an interesting way to tell the story."

CHAPTER 9

In 2000, J Mascis of fuzz rockers Dinosaur Jr went out on tour with former Minutemen bassist Mike Watt. Both huge fans of The Stooges, they proceeded to inject more and more Stooges material into their set until they were virtually playing just songs by their heroes. Hearing of the tour, Ron and Scott Asheton joined them on the road and a Stooges reunion of sorts was in progress.

J Mascis told the author of his fond memories of the tour coming together. "Let's see. I played with Mike Watt and he liked doing Stooges covers a lot. I did a show with him, doing Stooges covers. When I went on tour for my solo record, I got Watt to play bass and he would do a couple of Stooges covers. We played in Ann Arbor, and Mike knew Ron Asheton and invited him to the show. He came and jammed with us on a few Stooges shows. We invited him to a few more shows around the world. At All Tomorrow's Parties in LA, we were invited to play Stooges songs, and we got Scott Asheton. I guess that's when Iggy heard about it.

They told me that [I was a major factor in the eventual full Stooges reunion]. They were a big influence on me growing up. I listened to Ron a lot. The first Stooges album is my favourite guitar sound. I don't like James Williamson's sound so much. I like the songs, I just can't relate to it as much. I can play all of Ron's stuff, but I don't understand where James Williamson was coming from. I can't play any of his stuff. It doesn't come naturally to me. I don't like the sound as much. They were cool. Good guys. Scott's just a laid back guy."

Ron Asheton: "This is before Mike [Watt] would allow himself to have a cell phone. He doesn't want a leash. He calls his cellphone 'my leash and I don't like it'. He calls me up and says, 'Hey, we're playing in Ann Arbor. I'm playing with J Mascis & The Fog. We do some Stooges songs. Maybe you'd like to come down and play a couple of songs with us.' I go, 'Yeah, that sounds cool.' So I went down to the local rock place. I played at the end, what wound up being five songs. It was really fun. They were fun to play with. They had a day off, and the next day my girlfriend and I had a party. I said, 'I've had so much fun. If you ever want me to do this again, that'd be great.' Not too far down the road from there, it was South By Southwest and J calls up to ask me if I wanted to play it with them. Do the same thing, with Stooges songs at the end. That just continued on, wherever they could get a promoter to pony up for my expenses – because I wasn't really making any dough but I was having fun playing! We wound up playing Europe and doing All Tomorrow's Parties. We did a lot of cool jobs. It got to the point where J Mascis said 'Why don't we just go out and play a whole Stooges set?' So he hooked it up. We did All Tomorrow's Parties doing all Stooges, and a lot of the big festivals. That was really fun. Mike Watt sang. Mike could sing the songs. He has his own distinctive style. It's not Iggy but it was still rocking. They were great versions of those songs. I got Scotty in so we could have more Stooges. Then I go, 'Why are they billing this as a Stooges tribute show?' J goes, 'Yeah, why a tribute show when there's two from The Stooges in the band? It's not a tribute.' He got them to change it. I thought that was funnier than shit. That went as far as that could go and that was fun, and then that broke up because Mike had other things to do and J had The Fog. It was never meant to be anything other than trying to play as many shows as we could in a short time, and put some money in our pockets. We didn't make huge amounts but hey, it was enough to keep the boat floating."

When Iggy heard about the two Ashetons on tour playing a Stooges set, it sparked the idea in his mind of a full-on reunion. At the time, he was working on his *Skull Ring* solo album, and he invited the brothers into the studio to play on four tracks, 'Little Electric Chair', the title track of the album, 'Loser' and 'Dead Rock Star'. It's no coincidence that those four songs are the best on the album too. Like they'd never been apart, 'Little Electric Chair' is an upbeat song reminiscent of 'Fun House' or 'TV Eye'. *Skull Ring* too was to become a live favourite, with a classic, dirgey (sic) Ron Asheton riff running through Iggy's crooning.

Much of the rest of the album was recorded with Iggy's regular solo band, The Trolls, although there were other surprises too. Mega-selling pop punks Green Day appeared on two songs, 'Private Hell' and 'Supermarket', while even poppier punks Sum 41 guested on 'Little Know It All'. Repaying an earlier favour, rapper Peaches appeared on 'Rock Show'. The Stooge-less songs were far from bad, and *Skull Ring* is one of Iggy's finer 'solo' albums. But inevitably much of the press and attention went to those four Stooges songs, the first new material that the three men had recorded together since *Raw Power*. Ron Asheton also played bass on the recordings, filling in for Dave Alexander and reprising his *Raw Power* role, albeit in much happier circumstances.

Ron Asheton: "Those [J Mascis] shows were being so well accepted – people were excited just to see my brother and I. That was a good line-up of musicians. J Mascis was on the cover of *Rolling Stone*. People were interested, and we felt like it was getting closer. My brother's dream was always that The Stooges would get back together. I always hoped we would. I knew that Iggy had his own career and he was happy in it and he was doing well, so what the fuck … I'd just find something else to do.

Then I get that call. That fateful call. Iggy said, 'Hey, listen, I have this project, if you're interested.' He did say I could tell him 'no' outright, or I could listen to what he had to say. Or I could say no in two weeks or yes in two weeks or whatever. He left it open to me. I said, 'I love projects. I wanna do it. What is it?!' He laid out what became the *Skull Ring* CD. He goes, 'You can come down here with nothing or you can come down here with some music, whatever you want to do.' I thought about it and thought about it, and decided to go down with nothing. I wanted to go down and just see what happened when we got together. The night before we go down, I start to get scared. I decided that I needed an icebreaker, so I came up with the riff that became *Skull Ring*. Just something to kick it off. It worked too. It wound up being the icebreaker and getting on the record. It was really fun. We were only originally supposed to do two songs but we wound up doing four. Iggy was cool enough to just let me write songs on the spot. He goes, 'Here's what I'm gonna do. I'm gonna give you the studio for five hours in the afternoon and then I'll come in to see what's going on.' In those five hours, I'd already written what became 'Dead Rock Star' and 'Electric Chair'. I took a little riff that he had and turned that into 'Dead Rock Star'. He came down and they were already recorded, I'm already putting the bass on it, so things were jamming right along. It's fun working together and things are ploughing along. He was gracious enough to let us come to the mix. He didn't have to. While we were mixing, people started hearing that we had done this and we were back together. We weren't really back together, but then Iggy goes 'well hey, I got this call. The people from Coachella want us to play this festival.' He didn't know, but me and my brother were like 'Yes!' He was like, 'Well, I don't know.' He's very methodical and he kept going hot, cold, hot, cold. He goes, 'Well, I don't know. I don't like these one off reunion things. I just don't like it.' We thought, *Well, jeez, at least we'd get to fulfil part of a dream.* We got to get together to do the *Skull Ring* thing, and then play one big show. But I understand where he's coming from with just doing that one thing. He finally just said to us, 'You guys really wanna do this?' We're going 'Yeah.' So we did, and the rest is history."

Iggy's solo album would feature songs written and performed by The Stooges for the first time in a full 29 years. The record would prove to be a guinea pig, a test to see whether the three surviving members of the band would and could work together after so many years. Any doubts were soon extinguished when the band announced their first show together since their 'split' all those years before, at the Coachella Festival in 2003.

Iggy admits that, pre–*Skull Ring*, he didn't really consider calling up the Ashetons to play with him. "No, that's not the way I felt. That seemed like an impossible mess. What happened really was, well for one thing, the records I made in the 1970s, I was trying really hard to go out and play those songs with the band I recorded them with. That was the thing you did, so I was busy doing that, [so] the idea never came up. As I got into the mid-1980s [I] began establishing a liveable lifestyle as far as things that had nothing to do with music, like getting up in the morning, keeping accounts, paying the rent and all that. I associated the group with madness and obscurity. But I was missing the *feeling*. There was a drummer I had in the 1980s who was pretty gifted and had these drums that he could play at frightening speed, and he left me … to go with Rod Stewart. I thought, *Jeez Louise, what's going on?* I had some weird identity trouble there. By the early 1990s, I found myself hiring 'bad boys'. All of a sudden, it was Andy McCoy (Hanoi

Rocks), Alvin Gibb, Whitey Kirst and Pete Marshall, and it occurred to me, jeez aren't you basically redoing The Stooges here?! But my basic orientation at that point as a person was singular, solo, and I didn't really have what it took to pick up a group, which is basically a heavy barbell. About ten years later, I was in that position, around the early 2000s. I thought I could manage it, and it worked out swimmingly. That'd matured, and we were able to support each other in certain ways.

There were plants in the press. Thurston Moore [Sonic Youth] worked with them, and that guy from Seattle, Mark Arm [Mudhoney]. They were touting Ron. For the first time I was reading respected musicians saying that Ron was the better of the two guitarists in The Stooges, and that the James Williamson era was a wrong turn to them. Of course, I always felt that rock today is nothing if not politics. I felt that here was a group of people who could play a Ron Asheton riff but not a James Williamson riff. And why not? It's legitimate. They were getting to a point in their careers where, for various reasons, they wanted to rock. They didn't want to be entirely academic. They were gonna use Ron as a kind of touch point ... I thought that was great. People from David Bowie to Green Day do that with me all the time. That, together with the Mascis tour, put them on my radar. Suddenly, it didn't feel like picking something inert and gelatinous that had collected in a puddle somewhere in Detroit, Michigan. It now felt like something that was out there and was active. That's the way it is in this world.

I called Ron, it was still the same number. Someone had mentioned to me that they had seen him and he had said to them, 'I wish Jim would give a call.' So I thought, *OK that sounds like an open door.* I called him and I don't remember the ins and outs, but I didn't want to pressure him. I always thought of him as a good person, so I said, 'Look, there's something I'd like to do. It's on my record but it's with you. I don't know how you'd feel about that. Don't give me an answer now.' He said, 'I can give you an answer now – OK.' That was pretty much it. Then they came down and I remember seeing the two of them sitting kinda hulking, because they had both become very large fellows at that time! They're smaller now, but they had become very large in the interim. I met them in the twilight hours at a place called the Kent Hotel in the garden at Miami Beach and we were gonna go for dinner. They were sitting there, and to prove they were from Detroit, there were six or seven empty beer cans on the table in front of them. They were very quiet and cool, and we felt pretty comfortable hanging out. After that, we just got into it. At some point, we got offered this gig [Coachella]. I didn't want to do it unless they pony up and they did so I said to Ron and Scott, 'You wanna do this gig, straight split, share of the money, no funny business, no star power.' They said, 'Great' and that was about it."

Having had a fruitful time in the studio together, the stage was set for the band to spend some more time together on the road. They brought back Steve MacKay on sax, and coming in on bass was Mike Watt, dragged over from the J Mascis tour. Watt: "I met Ronnie first. He came to one of my gigs. It was either a Minutemen or a Firehose gig. It was a while back. He was a fan of my music. I don't want to sound self-important or anything, but he'd come and watch us and to me it was a mind blow, man. I loved The Stooges. We were teenagers in the 1970s when we first heard The Stooges and man, that guitar sound. He's a really nice cat. The whole trip, playing with them and everything, it's amazing. You don't expect shit like that."

For Watt it was a dream gig, The Stooges being such a big influence on his previous bands, Minutemen and Firehose. "Oh yeah. I don't even think there'd be a punk movement without them. They were like the common ground. So-Cal is like 150 towns, so when we met up in Hollywood, that was the one common ground thing. Everyone knew The Stooges. The Velvet Underground were also loved, but I can tell you for sure that everybody knew The Stooges. Everybody knew the songs. In those days, when they were putting out those records and for a little bit after, most people hated that stuff. But then the punk scene was full of weirdos anyway so it wasn't too far a stretch for them to be into it. But that was the one thing I noticed – that everyone knew them and was really into them."

Watt wasn't disappointed when he worked with the band either. "They're all interesting gentlemen. Iggy more about culture, Ronnie history, Scotty nature, Mackay politics. Because of the name and perhaps the simplicity of the music, you might think they were idiots.

Scott's more stoic. He's way into it, but I think being the younger brother, he has a different kind of role. But he's very enthusiastic; I probably spend more time with him on tour than anyone. He just doesn't wear it on his shirt sleeves so much. He's more of an inside man. He's a great spirit to play and he's got a lot of enthusiasm. The look on his [face] when he played – that's not intentional. That's not his spirit at all – he's a very up guy."

Watt stops short at calling himself a 'real' Stooge. "Y'know, Dave Alexander is the real Stooge. I think of him all the time. I'm there to learn and help those guys out as much as I can. I owe them my best notes and everything. I think it would be presumptuous of me to make that claim. I don't have the same history, the experiences … The Stooges is a lot about these guys coming together in the 1960s and really taking chances. I don't want to bum rush that."

Steve Mackay had been keeping in touch with what his former band mates had been doing, from a distance. "In the late 1970s and early 1980s, I saw Iggy perform a couple of times. At that stage though, it was pretty hard to get backstage and say hello to him. He had so many handlers and such. I was with Commander Cody, and we were leaving Atlanta when they were coming to Atlanta. That was actually the last time I spoke to him until he called me up to play Coachella. Even though I was fired, we remained friends. The Ashetons I would see from time to time when I was with the Violent Femmes, I'd come to town and they'd be there."

He himself was keeping busy. "I had a couple of versions of my own group, Carnal Kitchen. I played with Snakefinger for a while, most notably an album called *History Of The Blues*, which I believe is only available on vinyl – Rough Trade Deutschland. We did blues covers and I was the lead tenor sax player. That was a gruelling tour but a wonderful band, and it was a great pleasure to work with Philip Lithman. Me and my wife are friends with his daughter La-Ni Lithman to this day, and I stand in with her band Girls With Guns. I worked with Andre Williams for a couple of years on and off. I was with Commander Cody for about five years."

Mackay remembers first hearing about the reformation. "I had an inkling that something might be going on when I played with J Mascis And The Fog when they came to San Francisco. That was when I met Mike Watt, and my old pal Ronnie was playing with them. Right after that time, they went on to get Scott as the drummer so they had the core of The Stooges, minus Iggy. I think he was motivated by that. All of these other people were touring the Stooges songs. People had been asking him for years to put it back together. I remember Ronnie saying to me after having me sit in with them, 'We're sorry we don't have any money for you tonight, but something might be going on further down the line.' That turned out to be quite true. Several months later, I guess it was March or April 2003, he said, 'We're doing this thing down at Palm Springs. Do you want to do it?' I said, 'Yeah'. He said 'Do you need to rehearse?' I said, 'No.' So I didn't, I showed up, and I did the gig. I thought that even if nothing else came out of it, that was the greatest gig. The next thing you knew, we were going to New York, going to Spain, and now we're doing about forty-something shows [a] year!"

Backdoor Man writer, Tom Gardener: "I've seen them four times since they reformed, and they're quite good. Ron says that it's killing Iggy! He doesn't have to bounce around, he could just get up there and sing the songs. Nobody is gonna complain that loudly. The man's 60 years old and he deserves a break. He'd probably last a lot longer if he'd tone it down, but he's not gonna do that. It doesn't hurt having Mike Watt play bass. He's a fine bass player. Bringing back Steve Mackay to play sax is a nice touch."

Fellow *Backdoor Man* writer, Chris Marlow: "I was as sceptical as anyone about the reunion. I wouldn't have missed it for anything, but part of me was going, 'Please don't suck'. I was like 'Yay!' They were still really good.

They played a private gig here in LA and a girlfriend of mine had tickets. It wasn't a public show. It was for *Rocker Online*. A friend of mine brought me in as her plus 1, because she was covering it. It was totally not her kind of music, and about three songs in she turned to me and said, 'Would you mind very much if I left?' I said, 'Not as long as I can stay.' She took off. I told Ron and Iggy later, and Ron just started laughing. He goes, 'Yay, we still got it!' [They] still can affect people to the point where a very nice young woman actually had to leave the room. How many bands can say that? You just can't ignore them."

Scott Morgan: "At the reunion show [I saw], they were hitting on all cylinders. They're doing really good. What they need to do is learn how to translate their A+ live show into a record. Scott Asheton calls that 'letting it go'. Like when they're onstage jamming. They stop thinking about the song and just go for it. That's when things really start to take off in Scott's opinion and I think he's right. What they need to do is figure out how to do that in the studio, because I think that's what they were doing on the first Stooges album. Just jamming in the studio. Just letting it go where it wants to go."

After the reformed Stooges had played all over the world, including some high profile UK shows at the Download, Reading and All Tomorrow's Parties festivals, they stepped into the studio to record their first full length album together since *Raw Power* (an album totally omitted from The Stooges' set list during the tour, for obvious reasons).

The band picked Steve Albini as producer, previously a member of the bands Big Black, Rapeman and Shellac. His production CV featured the likes of Cheap Trick and Page & Plant, as well as more underground artists like Nirvana, Neurosis, PJ Harvey and Bush. His production on the new Stooges record, to be named *The Weirdness*, has been much maligned, but it's dirty and raw enough to work perfectly with the band.

Mike Watt: "He was like an engineer and he took total direction from those guys. Albini, like a lot of people from the punk era, had a lot of reverence for those guys. Like, I had a nightmare where there was this gravestone and all that was written on it was 'Fucked up the Stooges album'. I was so nervous about it, and it's the same with Albini. He wasn't heavy-handed at all.

Those guys would go to Florida and jam with Igg, come up with demos, then they'd float them to me and I'd learn the chords and everything. Igg would have me come to Miami in his little pad, and we went through every song. To me, it's such an honour to be on a Stooges record. Jesus."

Steve Mackay has his own feelings about the record. "I wish I had been involved in its production. I'm fairly happy with my contribution – I'm on four of the songs. Playing them live, I'm playing on a couple that I didn't play on the record, adding texture. I got a couple more solos handed to me. When I did the record they flew me in on one afternoon, I did three songs, the next day I did another song and then they flew me on to Nashville where I was hooking up with the Radon guys [a jazz band with an ever-rotating line-up, that Mackay has been involved in]. I wished I'd been there longer, but it was really great working with Steve Albini. I worked on one song just with him, and I learned a lot from him. I hadn't even heard the songs before

I went in there. Jim said, 'You're professional, you can do this.' The one song, 'Passing Cloud', nobody had heard before that day except for Scott and Iggy who had worked it up a couple of years before. I'm glad the record is getting a lot of attention. I've definitely never before been associated with a product that's gotten so much publicity about it. We do three or four songs from that album in the live show now."

The Weirdness was always going to suffer due to the fact that the previous three Stooges' albums are so revered, but taken at face value, it's an excellent piece of work that only enhances the band's reputation. Opener 'Trollin'' is a statement of the band's intent to return to the feel of the first two albums rather than the 'classic rock' sound on *Raw Power*. The manic 'My Idea Of Fun' was the song destined to become a live favourite, but it's on the title track that things really get interesting. Ron's whining riff and Mackay's muffled sax play over Iggy's crooning vocals on the record's slowest but perhaps most Stooges-like song.

Overall, the record was a success. Not all of the reviews agreed, but Manish Agarwal at *Mojo* gave it the credit that it deserved. "Steve Albini's tough, unvarnished recording doesn't try to modernise the quartet's elemental chemistry, ensuring that these twelve tunes pack an almighty sonic punch."

You could argue that this is reinventing the wheel, but that misses the point. *The Weirdness* is the sound of a working band, rock 'n' roll lifers doing what they need to do in the here and now. On those terms, The Stooges are still hard to beat."

Ron Asheton: "I like *The Weirdness* because nobody told us what we had to do. It was just fun. Albini's production is what it is. I like the tunes and I get a kick out of it. There will be another record though. We've talked about it."

Old friend Mique Craig is certainly glad to see them back. "You see so many groups coming back. I've seen the changes that Iggy's gone through. He cleaned himself up with drugs, then with his son and David Bowie. None of the guys do drugs anymore. They drink – Scott likes his beer and Ronnie drinks scotch or some kind of whisky. With the hard work they've done, it doesn't surprise me that they're successful now. They're no spring chickens anymore. They've gotta take life seriously. Ronnie lost his mama, less than two years ago. He still lives in that house. He's the only person I've ever known who lived with his mama his whole life. The only time he didn't live with her is when he lived out at Stooge Manor, and I think he went home a lot from there. He always had clean clothes on. His mom, Ann, was wonderful, a great lady. She always took care of him just like he was a little boy. He always had clean clothes and food in the house, and he didn't have to pay any rent. Scotty was the more ambitious one – he always wanted to get out and run around. All the girls were really hot for both of them back then, but Scotty's still got those good looks about him. Those beautiful blue eyes and long lashes. He's my sweetie. Scott's a wonderful guy … my daughter was working in a restaurant about a year ago, and Scott came in and said, 'How's Mique? How's your mom? Tell her I love her.' [I've been] having financial problems and living on social security, which is nearly nothing – I can barely buy groceries. He gave her [some money] and said, 'Tell your mom to buy herself something special.' That's the side of those guys that people don't see too much, unless you get close to them."

One man not getting together with his former band mates at the moment is James Williamson. "I really don't have any interest in doing that. But I have told them that, if they get into the rock 'n' roll hall of fame, I'd do that show! But I think that's highly unlikely at this point. They've been up for it, what, like seven times now? Every time, they get shot down. That's kinda part of being in The Stooges. We were always sort of an anti-establishment band. We weren't liked at the time and we still aren't. The Stooges are still pretty anti-establishment. The Ramones got in, but they were more commercial than us even though they acted like they weren't. We had no redeeming virtues whatsoever."

The band's singer is happy, if not 'comfortable'. "Comfortable is a word I wouldn't use," Iggy said to the author. "There are moments where personally I feel comfortable within the group, but I've never seen a good rock group yet that was a comfortable situation for the people in it. Musically, it's not a comfortable form of music, the medium. I do feel that we're one of the last. There just aren't people that do this any more. The groups that are major and what's called rock now – they don't really rock. And if they rock, they don't roll. They do different things for people, but they don't do what a rock 'n' roll group does. Right now, I've declared a few months off and I feel really good about that. I do feel that the events of the last four years with these guys make me keep coming back in my mind to the image of a salmon making that final leap upstream when it spawns. I kinda feel there was something I had to do to get to a certain point this group had to get to, in order to be 'in the book'. So we're in the book, and that's OK."

THE EROTICA BALL & CRUD

During a previous visit to Detroit, I had interviewed the female singer of an industrial punk band called Crud, a girl called Danielle, for Bizarre magazine. The friendship lasted the year, and so I saw a lot more of her when I went over on the Stooges trip. During that year, a friend of mine called Eric Hoegemeyer – who was the singer in the band Gold Cash Gold – had been taken on as the drummer in Crud. Suddenly my interest in the band was vast. When I was planning the Stooges trip, I noticed that Crud were to be performing at the first annual Detroit Erotica Ball, and I knew I had to be there because, though I loved the album Devil At The Wheel, I had never seen them play live. I didn't really know what I was letting myself in for.

I arrived at the venue (Bert's Warehouse, a legendary jazz club) early, at about 8pm. This is because I had gone straight from the People's Arts Festival earlier in the day, but it meant that I was early enough to grab myself a table and watch the various colourful characters arrive. There were people dressed head to toe in latex, there were transvestites (or transsexuals – I didn't get close enough to find out), there were doms with slaves on dog chains, and there were a fair few ordinary couples, out to titillate their wild sides. Bands like Syren and Broadzilla came and went, as did transgender folkie Stephanie Loveless. At 10pm, Eric arrived and we had a few drinks together, marvelling at just how much fun people could have when they were let off their leashes (no pun intended). It was all very sweet though – due to strict laws, the strippers had to wear sticky tape over their nipples. Erotica was in but nudity, it would seem, was a big no-no.

And then everything changed. At 11.30, half an hour before Crud's midnight set, Eric went backstage to prepare. I went to the bathroom but stopped in my tracks on my way there. On a love throne that some vendor was selling, two people were having sex. Full on, penetrative sex. Now, this wouldn't have been quite so shocking if not for the aforementioned strict laws. The performers on stage couldn't bare a nipple, and yet here were two

173

people going at it hammer and tong. And once they'd started, everyone seemed to pick up the baton (so to speak). It was impossible to go anywhere without seeing two people (or in some cases more than two) engaging in some sort of sexual activity. Girl on girl, girls on guy, the lot. The voyeur in me had disappeared after a very short while and the whole thing got a bit passé. But even I blinked when, during a conversation at a table with Danielle, I turned around and realised that the girl sitting to my immediate left had her hands down some guy's pants and she was tugging on him like she was trying to start a vintage car. Not only that, but the same guy had his mouth around her breast and she was goading him. So as I was trying to discuss music with my friend, all I could hear in my left ear was, "Yeah, suck it, you slut." Distracting, to say the least. But those are the lengths a good journalist is willing to go to in the name of research.

You're welcome.

Of course, The Erotica Ball is just the backdrop to the story of Crud, an excellent band formed by Sponge frontman Vinnie Dombroski. Sponge were a hugely successful alternative rock band that sprung out of Detroit in the 1990s and got some heavy MTV play. They supported the likes of Kiss, and seemed to be well on their way. However, despite their vast numbers of sales, they could never really command the respect that many people felt they deserved.

CONCLUSION

As I was coming to the end of writing this book, I made the decision to move to Detroit on a long-term basis. While researching the MC5 and The Stooges, the city and its surrounding area had such a profound impact on me that I couldn't think of anywhere I'd rather be. Of course, there was still a lot to sort out. I had to sell my flat in London, and I had to obtain some kind of working visa. I was told by Jerry Vile's *Essential Detroit* and the *Metro Times* paper that they'd give me some freelance work and I was going to be able to continue writing for the UK magazines that I was already connected with, but unfortunately this didn't guarantee me a visa. Still, my determination never let up and I wasn't in any doubt that I would end up living in Detroit. Over the course of my three visits, I had made so many friends that the place already felt like home, and the fact that my accent allowed me to punch two, maybe three, divisions above my weight with the ladies also didn't hurt.

With that decision made, the final couple of months of writing felt very different to the preceding four. I was working in earnest on a book about a band widely associated with the city of Detroit (even if, in all actuality, they're from the nearby city of Ann Arbor), while desperately trying to get my life in a position where I was able to move to the place. My determination to get there gave me a renewed focus with regards to this book. And there were many times when my enthusiasm had begun to flag. Ron and Scott Asheton, Iggy Pop and James Williamson had proved as yet elusive that, one month before deadline, the only members of The Stooges that I'd interviewed were sax man Steve Mackay and new bass player Mike Watt. Not that I'm playing down the importance of their contributions in any way, but I really needed to speak with the other boys if this was going to be taken seriously by Stooges fans. So it was a blessed relief when I was able to make contact with all of them. Ron told me that Scott hated doing interviews, but he would try to get him to talk to me, however briefly. I was convinced that, with his brother persuading him, Scott would come around.

In December of 2006, I attended the All Tomorrow's Parties Festival in Minehead. On the final day of the event, The Stooges and the reunited MC5 were playing together for the first time in decades. In fact, The Stooges would play before the 5 (now going under the name DKT/MC5), though that's a little misleading, as, on every night of the festival, a band would play at midnight after the headliner's set. Still, seeing The Stooges followed by the MC5 did feel like things had gone full circle. The Stooges played two sets that weekend but it was this final one that felt most special, especially when John Sinclair stepped out to introduce the MC5. Unfortunately, during The Stooges set when Iggy pulled his usual stunt of inviting the crowd up on stage with him, excitement got the better of me and I surfed to the security pit before ... falling in. My ankle took my full weight, and so I was faced with a very painful drive home to London. I vowed from then on to remember my age and that was destined to be my last ever crowd surf.

I've seen The Stooges six times since they reformed, watching them go from a band excited to be on stage together again playing those old songs to a genuine working rock 'n' roll band with artistic intentions, seamlessly slotting songs from *The Weirdness* in with the classics. As well as those two All Tomorrow's Parties sets, I also saw them at the Download Festival at Donington Park in 2004. Normally associated with metal bands like Slayer and Korn, The Stooges still seemed to be ideally placed on the main stage above punks The Distillers and Swedish garage kings The Hives. The Stooges were great that day too, pulling out all the stops and out-muscling bands a third of their age. Still, the Donington crowd didn't really take to them as they should have done; ironically, abominable nu-metalers Linkin Park went down a storm on the same day.

The following year, I went out to Lisbon in Portugal for the annual Super Bock Super Rock Festival. Spread over three days, this festival had the likes of New Order and Moby on the bill alongside metal titans like System Of A Down and Marilyn Manson. The Stooges played on the final day before headliner Manson and Audioslave. They were far better received by the Portuguese festival goers however, even though they played pretty much the same set.

A few months later and The Stooges were on the bill at the Reading Festival, playing on the final day after NOFX and before Marilyn Manson (again) and headliners Iron Maiden. The Brit metal legends were on fine form that day too, playing songs exclusively from their first three albums. But The Stooges ran them a close second despite, once again, playing the same set that they had been doing since the reformation.

By the time they got to All Tomorrow's Parties two years later, *The Weirdness* was recorded if not released and the band began to introduce more new songs into the set. As well as the DKT/MC5, they shared the bill with Detroit hardcore band Negative Approach, Gang Of Four, Dinosaur Jr, Melvins and Sonic Youth (whose founding member Thurston Moore was the curator of the event) that weekend.

At the time of writing, my most recent Stooges show was during the summer of 2007 at the legendary Glastonbury Festival. The weekend had its traditional rain storm and the event was little more than a washout, with people struggling against the weather and the resulting mud in order to get anywhere. On the Saturday, former Jam man Paul Weller played a set on the Pyramid Stage before I trudged through the filth to see former Creedence Clearwater Revival singer John Fogerty on the Jazz/World Stage. Finally, after another mud-walk, I got to the Other Stage to see

The Stooges perform a headline set. They weren't at their absolute best that day, but they were certainly the better option to The Killers, who were headlining over on the Pyramid. Weeks before Glastonbury, Mike Watt said to me that, "That's big all over the world. It's the big daddy. I love all The Stooges' gigs but that'll be new for me."

I always knew that this book would receive some criticism due to the amount of Iggy Pop biographies already available. Despite making it clear that this book is about The Stooges as a band and not just about Iggy, and that I was in fact focussing on the other members of the band more than the singer, I'm still sure that this will be the case. But that's OK, because I believe that genuine fans of the band will understand what I have set out to achieve here. That said, it was still important for the integrity of any book about The Stooges to at least speak with the infamous frontman. He eventually called me just one week before deadline, and though that fact had me biting my nails throughout November and the early part of December 2007, in retrospect I wouldn't have it any other way. It's perfect. And when I did speak with him, he was an absolute pleasure. Funny, sharp and charming, Iggy showed me no signs of the ego that some people had led me to believe he has.

As the title suggests, my intention was to take you on a journey through Michigan so that you, the reader, can see where this band came from while I'm telling the story. You can also track my research trip and the many ridiculous places and experiences that it took me through. The title is a double-edged sword. This book tells of the band's journey, and my own while trying to find out about them. This was a frustrating book to write in many ways, but it was also a lot of fun. It was certainly a unique experience, and as I sit wondering exactly what I'm going to start work on now, I'm convinced the next six months will be nothing like the last six.

Meanwhile, The Stooges will keep touring, and they're planning another album. Lord knows, the world is a more exciting place with them in it. Who knows how long it will hold together, but it's that unpredictability that makes them all the more thrilling. There are few better rock 'n' roll bands in existence right now, and for a band that had been apart for thirty years, that's a hell of an achievement. Long may it continue.

DISCOGRAPHY

THE STOOGES

The Stooges (1969, Elektra)
Fun House (1970, Elektra)
Raw Power (1973, Columbia)
Metallic K.O. (1976, Jungle)
Heavy Liquid box set (2005, Easy Action)
Telluric Chaos (2005, Jungle)
The Weirdness (2007, Virgin)

DVDs
Live In Detroit (Pias Recordings, 2004)
Escaped Maniacs (Liberation Entertainment, 2007)

IGGY POP

The Idiot (Virgin, 1977)
Lust For Life (Virgin, 1977)
Kill City (Bomp, 1977 – featuring James Williamson)
TV Eye Live (Virgin, 1978)
New Values (Arista, 1979)
Soldier (Arista, 1980)
Party (Arista, 1981)
Zombie Birdhouse (Arista, 1982)
Blah Blah Blah (A&M, 1986)
Instinct (A&M, 1988)
Brick By Brick (Virgin, 1990)

America Caesar (Virgin, 1993)
Naughty Little Doggie (Virgin, 1996)
Avenue B (Virgin, 1999)
Beat Em Up (Virgin, 2001)
Skull Ring (Virgin, 2003 – featuring four Stooges tracks)

RON ASHETON

As The New Order
The New Order (Isadora, 1977)

As Destroy All Monsters
Bored (Cherry Red, 1999)

As Dark Carnival
Live – Welcome To Show Business (Vivid, 1990)
Greatest Show In Detroit (Vivid, 1991)
Last Great Ride (Sympathy For The RI, 1997)

Destroy All Monsters/Dark Carnival
Hot Box box set (Lost Patrol)

SCOTT ASHETON

Scott Morgan
Rock Action (Revenge, 1990)
Scot's Pirates (School Kids, 1994)
Revolutionary Means (School Kids, 1996)]

As Sonny Vincent
Shotgun Rationale (Vince Lombardy High School Records, 1993)

Pure Filth (Overdose, 1997)
Hard In Detroit (Nest Of Vipers, 1998)
Parallax In Wonderland (Devil Doll, 2000)
The Good, The Bad, The Ugly (Acetate, 2003)

As The Farleys
Youth In Asia (Farleys, 2001)
Meet The Stooges (Farleys, 2001)

BIBLIOGRAPHY

Iggy Pop: Open Up And Bleed – Paul Trynka (Sphere)

Gimme Danger: The Story Of Iggy Pop
– Joe Ambrose (Omnibus Press)

Grit, Noise And Revolution: The Birth Of Detroit Rock 'N' Roll
– David A. Carson (University Of Michigan Press)

From The Velvets To The Voidoids: The Birth Of American Punk Rock – Clinton Heylin (Helter Skelter)

Please Kill Me: Uncensored Oral History Of Punk
– Legs McNeil (Abacus)

Bowie: Loving The Alien – Christopher Sandford (Time Warner)

Strange Fascination: David Bowie – David Buckley
(Virgin Books)

EXTRACTS FROM THE AUTHOR'S

'DETROIT DIARIES — STOOGES TRIP' (SEPTEMBER 2007)

Friday 14th
Smooth flight, landed at 5.30pm Detroit time. Picked up my
luggage and car, and drove to Steve Zuccaro's (Gold Cash Gold)
place. Unpacked, then got picked up by his friends Becca and
Stephanie and drove to Royal Oak where we met with my
friends Eric Hoegemeyer and Dave Alison. Had a few drinks,
then drove to the Majestic Café where we met with Hedda
Hart, another old friend from past visits. Drank some more, then
finished at the Tap Room, my favourite Detroit bar. Drank more,
then went back to Steve's where we met some guys from a hip-
hop band called the Dub Phonics. Turned in at about 4am.

Saturday 15th
After getting breakfast at a great little greasy spoon called Janet's
Lunch, I went to the Russell Industrial Centre, where the
People's Arts Festival was being held. Got there at about 11am,
just as it was starting. Saw some great bands (The Detroit Silver
Tones, Quixotic, The Loftees w/Johnny Chrome, Nicholas J.
Fugedi, Jill Jack, Johnny Mundane & The Sweet Spots and Audra
Kubat, an old friend of Times Beach Records) and some not so
great bands including one that just played bass to backing tapes).
There was also a movie projector set up, showing arty shorts,
including Leni Sinclair's *Kick Out The Jams* film. There were a
heap of artistic vendors, and I renewed acquaintances with some
old friends and people that have helped me out in the past.
Robert Stanzler, who used to run Made In Detroit, was there
with his new company Detroit Manufacturing. Leni Sinclair was
there and she introduced me to Rob Tyner's wife Becky. I gave

her a copy of my MC5 book, and I really hope she likes it. I met Len Beste, who had been helping me with information online. I met Johnny Bee, who has played with everyone including Alice Cooper on the *Welcome To My Nightmare* album. I met artists Mark Arminski and Carl Lundgren, photographer Michael Spleet and Gary Grimshaw's wife Laura, plus guys from the HellCity and Full Effect labels. A good day.

I left at 7pm and, after grabbing a White Castle, went straight to the Detroit Erotica Ball at Bert's Warehouse. Again some great bands played (Syren, MT-TV, Overloaded, Broadzilla, Tyranny, Konniption Fit and Stephanie Loveless). Nothing could prepare me for the night ahead though. My buddy Eric's band Crud headlined (and rocked the place to the ground).
I also bumped into another old friend Karen from Queen Bee. It was cool to see her.
I met a great photographer called Miss Shela too,
All in all, a great, if slightly debauched and very fucked up, night.

Sunday 16th
Another crazy busy day. I chilled out all morning (went back to Janet's Lunch for an omelette), and then at 2.30 made my way to Ford Field to see the Detroit Lions take on the Minnesota Vikings (American Football). The game kicked off at 4.05, and I got a £62 ticket for $40 from a tout, 29 rows from the front. It was a great seat. The game was amazing too. After the fourth quarter, the score was 17 each (Vikings missed a last minute field goal, hitting the post, that would have won it for them) and it went into overtime. First team to go ahead wins. Detroit won it with a field goal and the place went crazy. Amazing.
After that, I went to see funk legend George Clinton with Eric at the Royal Oak Theatre. We had a drink at Ronin first. George was cool. He played 'Atomic Dog' and a cover of Creedence's

'Proud Mary'. He has a tight band. It was cool to see a Detroit legend in Detroit. Went to the Tap Room afterwards.

Monday 17th

My interview with Niagara from Destroy All Monsters was moved until tomorrow, so instead I headed on over to the old Grande Ballroom. It's a messed up old building now, and it's kind of sad. But I was still in awe of what went on in that place. And there's some cool MC5 graffiti on the walls. I took some great pictures.

In the evening I met up with Eric and we went to see Rilo Kiley at the Royal Oak Theatre, supported by Johnathan Rice. Rice was OK, but Rilo Kiley were amazing. The singer, Jenny Lewis (a former child star), has an incredibly beautiful voice. Great show. Afterwards, we went to Gusoline Alley, a great little dive bar with an amazing jukebox, for a few drinks. Met Scott Ross, an old friend who used to road manage Gold Cash Gold. Scott thinks he can hook me up with some contacts, for magazine work and for Stooges. Also re-met Paul Randolph from the Harper Woods Heroes. Met for the first time Jimmy Doom (The Almighty Lumberjacks Of Death) and Shakey, an apparently brilliant drummer. Another cool night.

Tuesday 18th

I met with Scotty Ross at noon and discussed a few business opps, including possibly doing some work for *Clear Magazine*. At 4pm, I met with Niagara from Destroy All Monsters, and her chap The Colonel. We met at the Majestic Café. She was kinda wonderful and they both filled me with stories. Niagara gave me a book and they think they can set me up with Ron Asheton so it could all be worth it.

Had a quiet evening at the Tap Room.

Wednesday 19th

Went to the Rock Stars Cars & Guitars exhibition at the Henry Ford Museum this morning. Saw cars belonging to Kiss, Bob Seger, Metallica, Marilyn Manson, etc. Guitars belonging to Cheap Trick, ZZ Top, etc. Pretty cool stuff.
Another quiet evening. Hung out at Gusoline Alley with Trazey and Gary, who I'd met on Myspace.

Thursday 20th

In the morning, I met with Russ Gibb from the Grande Ballroom at Dimitri's diner in Dearborn. He's a sweet guy, and he told me a few stories.
In the evening, I went to see the movie *It's A Detroit Thing*, all about the music scene in the East side over the past 15 years. It covered Stun Gun and Queen Bee, featuring my friends Danielle and Karen. Also went to the pre-show and after-show parties. Finished the evening at Rustbelt studio listening to tracks with Eric and Danielle.

Friday 21st

Very quiet day, just chilled out then went to the Tap Room at night. Back to Hedda's friend Melissa's place after that.

Saturday 22nd

In the afternoon, went to Jerry Vile's art opening at the Bohemian National Home Gallery. Later on, went to the *Detour Magazine* launch party at the Majestic. Handed out cards to the magazine people, and saw The Hadituptoheres (great), Freer (bad), KO & The Knockouts (OK) and Bulldog (amazing).

Sunday 23rd

Met with Dino (Gold Cash Gold) for brunch, with Steve. Watched the Lions get whooped on TV.

In the evening, I drove out to Ann Arbor to see Ani DiFranco at the Michigan State Theatre. Great show and well worth the drive. Went back to Steve's afterwards, parked up and walked to the Tap Room. Drank far too much.

Monday 24th

I went to Niagara and Colonel's place today. Had a great barbeque and asked Niagara some more questions. I really like them. They gave me a shirt, some *Punk* and *Juxtapose* magazines, a signed Dark Carnival print and a Destroy All Monsters/Dark Carnival boxed set. Great afternoon.

Afterwards, went to see the new Rob Zombie version of *Halloween*. It was OK, but went with Danielle from Crud so it was extra fun.

After that, we both went to Gusoline Alley and met with Eric. Had a few drinks then went home.

Tuesday 25th

Met with Johnny B from Detroit Wheels/Alice Cooper today at his house and got some great stories. Also went to photographer Richard Peardon's house and he gave me a great Stooges print. Went to see the Tigers beat the Minnesota Twins 8-0 at Comerica Park with Danielle. Met Eric there too. Great game – we kicked ass.

Then, went to the Magic Stick to see The Black Lips play. All in all, an awesome day.

Wednesday 26th

Had a lazy day, just setting up some interviews.
Later on, went to watch Danielle bowl and ended up bowling myself as there was a no-show. I did alright – got a 103 which was better than the no-show average of 90. Great, great fun.

Thursday 27th

Met with Jerry Vile from The Boners/*Orbit* magazine today. Had an amazing day. I picked him up at his place, then we went to Marvin's Mechanical Museum, which is like an old arcade with crazy, sinister looking anatomical figures and stuff. Like that sailor that laughs when you give him a quarter. I played Jerry at *Simpsons* pinball but didn't really work out who won. I think he did. We then had a drink and some cheese fries at a bar close by and I did the interview. Finally, we went to a rummage sale at a church, which was maybe more bizarre than Marvin's place. There was a heap of trash for sale, and then a sectioned off part of 'special goods'. We queued to get in, and it was just more trash. Funny. I bought some crap – two t-shirts, a Michigan sweater and a Detroit board game. All that cost $5 (£2.50). That night, I went to see The Heart Attacks at Smalls with Danielle and Eric, then got stoned.

Friday 28th

Interviewed Ron Cooke from the Sonic's Rendezvous Band today. He was cool. I met with him at his house in Ann Arbor. Went to see the Subhumans at the Magic Stick with Eric, Steve and Danielle that night. Cool show, but it was great to hang out with my fave Detroiters on my last night. Went to a Funk Club at the Bohemian National Home Gallery afterwards. Fun place with some great music. Bad dancing though.

Saturday 29th

Went to a mall. First shopping I did in two weeks. Saw Steve, Ashley and Dan before I left. Had a close call coming home as there were nearly no seats and I was flying standby, but one guy didn't show and had his luggage taken off the plane.

PRAISE FOR MC5: SONICALLY SPEAKING

"Brett Callwood's new book spills the beans with first-hand interviews and an enthusiastic take on their incredible career from revolution and imprisonment, to drugs, death and glorious reformation." *Jo Kendall, Kerrang!*

"The only band who ever disturbed the smug equanimity of The Who back in the early Grande days. I will enjoy the inside story." *Pete Townshend, The Who*

"All MC5 aficionados and rock fans worldwide absolutely *must* read this book. Through interviews with the surviving members and a host of others, the past gets placed in excellent perspective to the present. Great job!"
Dennis Thompson, MC5 drummer

"When I was talking with Brett Callwood about my time in the MC5, it reminded me that when we were in the middle of creating whatever it was that we created, we became a circle of five that was really one. Nobody could penetrate that circle, not even the people that we lived with. Callwood does a great job of letting the reader into the circle for a look around."
Michael Davis, MC5 bassist

"Callwood has done a great job of providing an excellent rendition of an amazing story, and it's high time too."
Paul Raggity, Rock Sound (8/10)

"The book paints a picture of a hectic and somewhat controversial start to the MC5's career, with edgy stage stunts and crowd clashes. Essentially, it is another read that romanticizes the sixties, making you wish you were around when it all happened... his passion instils a sense of enthusiasm and makes this a thoroughly enjoyable read." *Jas Grieve, Big Cheese (4/5)*

"The MC5 were always much more that a band with great tunes and Brett Callwood realises that. This book documents the music, the politics and the attitude of the greatest band ever to come out of the motor city and is a definite buy for anybody who wants to know where punk really started!!!!" *Diamond Dave, Total Rock Radio*

"*Sonically Speaking* is essentially a story of a potentially great and innovative group that burned bright for a brief moment and then self-destructed, and gained that dubious legendary status many years later after the tragic deaths of their two key members." *Pete Makowski, Classic Rock (7/10)*

"Their legacy and influence far outweighs their short career and Brett's passion for the band shines through every page." *Geoff Nicholls, Rhythm (4/5)*

"Brett Callwood has written – and written well – the long-awaited definitive biography of the MC5, nailing down the important information in the correct order, paying close attention to the actual facts as opposed to accepted myths and legends, and telling the true story of the MC5 from beginning to end. If I enjoyed it this much, how you think you gonna like it?" *John Sinclair, former MC5 manager*

"It's an eminently readable tome that, aside from anything else, may make you think twice before rolling a comforting doobie..." *Guitarist*

"Callwood has picked up the challenge, producing an objective insight into the men who were the MC5 and their immediate entourage. It's to his credit that he's not only talked to the remaining members of the band but key figures like former manager John Sinclair."
Malcolm Dome, Metal Hammer (8/10)

"Sincere and straightforward." *Iggy Pop*

ALSO
AVAILABLE

FROM

INDEPENDENT MUSIC PRESS

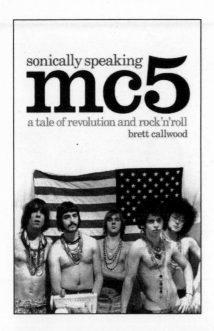

MC5: SONICALLY SPEAKING – A TALE OF PUNK ROCK AND REVOLUTION
by **Brett Callwood**

The first in-depth biography of the group, Sonically Speaking charts the career of this most seminal of bands, as well as unravelling what became of the members after the break up of the MC5. For this definitive book, author Brett Callwood travelled to Detroit and Los Angeles to track down and interview the three surviving founder members of the MC5 in-depth. He also spoke at length with other key players in this remarkable tale, such as former manager John Sinclair, artist Gary Grimshaw, former White Panther Pun Plamondon, Leni Sinclair, Jackson Smith – the son that MC5's Fred had with Patti Smith – and Russ Gibb, manager of the legendary Grandee Ballroom, among others.

ISBN 0 9552822-2-5 224 Pages Paperback, 12 b/w pics £12.99 World Rights

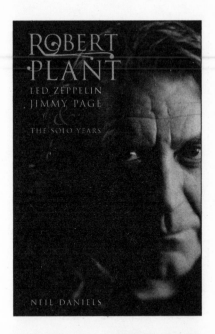

ROBERT PLANT: LED ZEPPELIN, JIMMY PAGE & THE SOLO YEARS
by Paul Stenning

Robert Plant is a genuine rock legend. Amazingly, thirty years on, his star continues to shine. The tale of Led Zeppelin is central to his life, but that ended at the close of the Seventies – and Plant has been recording new music almost constantly in the 25 years since. For the first time, his solo years – working with his former Led Zep cohort Jimmy Page, numerous guest appearances and his own material – are covered in depth in a biography. With Led Zeppelin he conquered the world, with a close and continuing partnership with Zeppelin six-stringer Jimmy Page he straddled the boundaries of rock, blues and metal; the likes of Dreamland, a relatively obscure batch of cover songs, pay homage to Plant's earliest and ongoing influences and passions such as deep blues and classic R&B; the book also places Plant's later work in the wider context of both Led Zep's own legacy and the broader history of modern music. This is the very first book to tell the complete story of a poor young kid from West Bromwich who belied his humble blues roots by becoming one of the most recognisable rock superstars.

ISBN 0-9552822-7-6 ISBN 978-0-9552822-7-0 224 Pages
Paperback, 8pp b/w pics £12.99 World Rights

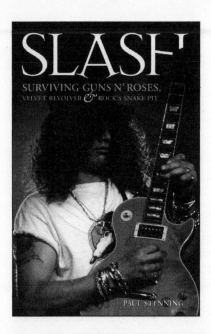

SLASH: SURVIVING GUNS N' ROSES, VELVET REVOLVER & ROCK'S SNAKE PIT
by Paul Stenning

A human cartoon of hair, super-strength cigarettes and the rock world's most famous top hat, Slash is one of the most iconic guitarists in recent memory. Although born in Stoke-on-Trent, this one-off guitarist came to prominence through the debauchery and stellar chart success of the American west coast's Guns N' Roses; Slash's highly productive but volatile relationship with lead singer Axl Rose led to a perhaps inevitable split in the mid-90s. Moving on first to his own Snakepit project, then a blues band, then on to a career as one of the world's most sought after soloists, Slash's profile has finally returned to its highest peak with the formation of the outrageous and hugely successful Velvet Revolver, a super-group of rock stars that lives life as hard as his former band-mates ever did.

His story is inevitably one of massive rock and roll excess, exhausting and famous live shows, fiery confrontations with other musicians but also of incredible discipline, a unique natural musical gift and, of course – through 'Sweet Child O' Mine' and 'Paradise City' to name but a few – the creation of some of rock music's most legendary songs.

ISBN: 0-9552822-3-3 ISBN 978-0-9552822-3-2 224 Pages
Paperback, 8pp b/w pics £12.99 World Rights

BRUCE DICKINSON: FLASHING METAL WITH IRON MAIDEN AND FLYING SOLO
by Joe Shooman

Bruce Dickinson is best known as frontman for the multi-million selling giants of heavy metal, Iron Maiden, with whom he has enjoyed worldwide success for 25 years. However, his story outside of Maiden is equally remarkable. Prior to joining that band in 1981 for their seminal, multi-million selling *Number Of The Beast* LP – one of the most influential records in the history of Heavy Metal – Dickinson enjoyed stardom with fellow New Wave Of British Heavy Metal artists Samson, while his post-Maiden solo career has brought much critical success. Further away from his day job, Dickinson is a true renaissance man. A world-class fencer and member of the British Fencing team, he also hosts his own show on flagship digital radio station, BBC 6Music, is a best-selling fiction author, a keen military historian, and TV presenter for the Discovery Channel and Sky One. Dickinson is also employed by the commercial airline Astreus as a first officer, when his bulging Maiden schedule allows, and even participated in a mercy mission to rescue British residents from Beirut during 2006. This book tells his story for the first time, through exclusive interviews with those who know him best: from his formative days straddling the upsurge of the New Wave of British Heavy Metal, all his time in Maiden, through his solo years and the many extra-curricular projects he loves, right up to the present day, where Iron Maiden are rightly considered legends of music worldwide.

ISBN 0-9552822-4-1 ISBN 978-0-9552822-4-9 224 Pages
Paperback, 8pp b/w pics £12.99 World Rights